PREPARE

WORKBOOK WITH DIGITAL PACK

Helen Chilton   **Second Edition**

B1

LEVEL 5

Cambridge University Press
www.cambridge.org/elt

Cambridge Assessment English
www.cambridgeenglish.org

Information on this title: www.cambridge.org/9781009032124

© Cambridge University Press and Assessment 2015, 2019, 2021

First published 2015
Second Edition 2019
Second Edition update 2021

20 19 18 17 16 15 14

Printed in Dubai by Oriental Press

A catalogue record for this publication is available from the British Library

ISBN   978-1-009-03212-4   Workbook with Digital Pack
ISBN   978-1-009-03211-7   Student's Book with eBook
ISBN   978-1-009-03213-1   Teacher's Book with Digital Pack

CONTENTS

1 GOING SHOPPING

1 Match the words to their meanings.

1 charge
2 customer service
3 discount
4 exchange
5 online shopping
6 promotion
7 purchase
8 receipt
9 refund
10 send something back

a a piece of paper you receive when you buy something
b money given back to you if you return something
c take something back to a shop and replace it with something else
d something that you buy
e helping customers in a polite way
f ask for money for a service or activity
g a special offer on a product
h shopping on the internet
i return an item that you bought online
j a lower price than usual for something

2 Choose the correct answer.

1 The *customer service / online shopping* is excellent in this shop. They're really helpful to customers.
2 I saw an advertisement yesterday about a 20% *refund / discount* on all electrical items.
3 If the shorts don't fit, you can always *send them back / refund them.*
4 How much did you *shop / spend* on that new game?
5 I've lost the *refund / receipt,* but perhaps you have the information on your computer system.
6 When you work in a shop, you have to do more than just *serve / charge* customers.
7 There are some great *exchanges / promotions* at M&F – you can buy one item and get one free!
8 The watch shop doesn't *charge / spend* you if you need a new battery.
9 The sales assistant said that I could get a *receipt / refund* if I brought the jumper back within 30 days.
10 You don't always have to pay delivery *charges / receipts* when you shop online.

3 Complete the sentences with the words in the box. There are two words you do not need.

| charge | discounts | exchange | online |
| receipt | refund | served | spends |

1 The shop gave me a _____ when I paid for my T-shirt.
2 Get to BooksForAll now! We have amazing _____!
3 Have you ever done any _____ shopping?
4 The boy who _____ us is in Year 12.
5 I'd like to _____ these jeans for these trousers, please.
6 Monica _____ a lot of money on clothes.

4 Complete the sentences so that they are true for you.

1 I spend about _____ on clothes per month.
2 I love shopping for _____ but I hate shopping for _____.
3 In my country, they charge us to go into _____.
4 The last thing that I sent back was _____.

1 You are going to read an article about a shopping centre called the Dubai Mall. Read the article quickly. What's special about the mall?

The BIGGEST shopping centre in the world

Dubai is an amazing place to go shopping and if you love fashion, this is the place to come! My favourite place is the Dubai Mall. It's the largest shopping centre in the world by total area and there are about 1,200 shops. There are different 'districts' in the mall. For example, there's one whole section which sells shoes, and another which sells jewellery. I often spend time walking up and down Fashion Avenue with my friends – that's where the designer shops are, like Dolce & Gabbana and Dior. ¹ _____ It's great to look in the windows at the luxury items, though.

Some people think shopping malls are boring, but the Dubai Mall isn't! Of course, there are a lot of shops, but there are plenty of other things to see and do there. There's an aquarium and underwater zoo, and we go to the cinema or ice-skating there, as well. ² _____ You need them because it's pretty easy to get lost!

There are a lot of places to eat in the mall. ³ _____ There's fast food, many different kinds of international food, and healthy stuff, too. I love going to the Rainforest Café. We usually get fruit smoothies and burgers. There's one called the 'Jungle Chicken Burger', which is delicious. The desserts are great. I love seeing little kids' faces when the 'Sparkling Volcano' dessert arrives at their table. It's a huge chocolate thing! ⁴ _____

Next to the mall is the Burj Khalifa – the tallest building in the world. You can travel up to the observation deck at the top of the building from the mall. From there you can look down on Dubai. I don't go up there very often because everything looks so small from above that you can't see it very well. I go to the Dubai Fountain several times a year, though. ⁵ _____ It's the world's largest musical fountain and it's free to watch. It's fun!

 PREPARE FOR THE EXAM

Reading Part 4

2 **Five sentences have been removed from the text below. For each question, choose the correct answer. There are three extra sentences which you do not need to use.**

A You can get anything you like.
B They charge a lot of money to do this.
C We can't afford to buy much there, even when there are discounts or promotions.
D That's just outside the mall, too.
E Sometimes my friends and I share one.
F My favourite one is a new skirt I bought.
G I don't but my friends sometimes do.
H There are customer service desks, too, where you can ask for directions.

 EXAM TIPS

• Read the text quickly to get a general idea of what it is about. Ignore the gaps for now.
• Choose the best sentence (A–H) for each gap, and when you have chosen all the answers, read through the whole text again to check it makes sense.

3 **Match the highlighted words and phrases in the article to the meanings.**

1 expensive, comfortable or beautiful
2 one of the parts that something is divided into
3 an area that has a special character which makes it different from others
4 another word for a shopping centre
5 how big something is

GRAMMAR Determiners

1 Choose the correct word.

1 Last week my parents visited _____ shops.
   a no   **b** any   **c** several
2 They wanted to buy _____ computer games for my brother and me.
   a much   **b** some   **c** plenty
3 There are so _____ games to choose from.
   a much   **b** many   **c** a lot of
4 They asked the shop assistant _____ questions.
   a any   **b** plenty   **c** a lot of
5 He said that there weren't _____ action games in the shop at the moment.
   a plenty   **b** any   **c** several
6 There were _____ car race games either.
   a much   **b** plenty   **c** no
7 There was an animal game, but he didn't think it would be _____ fun for me.
   a no   **b** much   **c** many
8 But then they looked online and they found _____ of games to choose from.
   a plenty   **b** several   **c** some

2 Complete the conversation with the words from the box. Use each word once only.

a lot of	any	many	much	no
plenty	several	some	some	

A: Hi! Can I help you?
B: Yes, I'd like [1] _____ information about an extra piece of equipment I need for my mobile phone.
A: OK, which one? We have [2] _____ extras here!
B: My friend said that there are [3] _____ batteries that last a long time between charging them. I have a battery at the moment but it lasts hardly [4] _____ time at all.
A: Well, it depends what you do with your phone. [5] _____ battery lasts forever!
B: I know, but my friend said it gives [6] _____ charges.
A: Ah, I know! It's called a power box, I think. I've got them in [7] _____ of different colours.
B: That's it. How [8] _____ power does it have?
A: I think it has three charges in it. I have a more expensive model that has [9] _____ more charges – about 20 I think.
B: No, I think that three is enough. Thanks! I'll take it!

3 Choose the correct sentence in each pair.

👁 1 **a** Do you have free time on Saturday?
    b Do you have any free time on Saturday?
2 **a** My brother spends much money on clothes.
    b My brother spends a lot of money on clothes.
3 **a** Ben bought two shirts and some jeans.
    b Ben bought two shirts and jeans.
4 **a** I have so much shoes!
    b I have so many shoes!
5 **a** If you have any questions, talk to customer services.
    b If you have some questions, talk to customer services.

VOCABULARY any

1 Match the questions to the answers.

1 Where are my shoes?
2 How are you feeling today?
3 What's the matter with your phone?
4 Did you get Mark's present?
5 Can I borrow that, please?
6 Where's Marcia?
7 Why was he shouting at you?

a I have no idea. I haven't done anything wrong.
b No, there wasn't anything suitable.
c This app isn't any good.
d I haven't seen them anywhere.
e I don't know. Has anyone seen her this morning?
f You can have it! I don't want it any more.
g Not any better, really.

2 Choose the correct answer.

1 I haven't made *anything / any good* for dinner yet.
2 Emily Johnson isn't at our school *any longer / any good.* She moved last term.
3 This film isn't *any more / any good* – let's watch something different.
4 Has *anyone / any* got a pen?
5 There isn't *anything / anywhere* in the fridge. Can we go out for dinner?
6 My test results this term weren't *any good / any better* than last term.
7 Leonardo Di Caprio still hasn't won *anything / any* Oscars.
8 I don't mind where we go – *anywhere / anything* away from here!

1 Read the title of the article. Where do you think the three teenagers in the article like shopping most? Read the article quickly and check your ideas.

My **favourite** place to shop

We asked three teenagers where they like shopping most. Here's what they said.

Maggie, 15 Most of my friends shop online for new fashions, but I'm actually into vintage stuff – second-hand clothes from different periods, like the 1960s. I've got some awesome boots and a few dresses from that time. You have to go to specialist shops to get stuff like that. Fortunately, I live in an area where there's a huge vintage market at the weekend with tons of amazing stalls. You can find online shops that sell vintage clothing, too, but I prefer to try things on before I buy them.

Özkan, 16 I'm always on my phone looking at stuff online. I collect watches. Well, to be honest, I collect information about watches! I can't afford to buy any myself yet, but my aunt and uncle bought me a really cool watch for my birthday and it's made me really interested in unusual ones from around the world. One day I'd like to be a collector but for now, I'll just keep browsing. I download apps from a site called AppIt, which has got tons of brilliant stuff!

Gem, 17 I don't spend a lot of money, but when I've got some, I go down to the big department store in town. It's fantastic – there are sections for everything, from clothes and shoes to phones and food. It's great! I just walk around looking at stuff. I do buy small things when there are special offers, like make-up or hair products, but mainly I just look – 'window shopping' they call it! It's fun, and there's a cute café on the top floor, where I go for coffee with my friends.

2 Find adjectives in the article which describe the following:

1 something to wear on your feet (text 1) ....
2 a place where you can buy things in a market (text 1) ....
3 something which helps you tell the time (text 2) ....
4 goods you can buy online (text 2) ....
5 a large shop where you can buy a lot of different things (text 3) ....
6 a place where you can have something to eat and drink (text 3) ....

3 Where's your favourite place to buy things and why? How would you describe it? Think about what you can find or do there and make some brief notes.

4 Write about your favourite place to shop. Include some of the adjectives from the texts in Exercise 1. Write about 80 words. Remember to check your spelling and grammar.

2 BEST FRIENDS FOREVER

1 Complete the crossword, using the clues on the right.

This describes someone who

1 is reasonable and has good judgement.
2 wants something that somebody else has.
3 always supports and likes someone.
4 has a natural skill for something.
5 worries about things.
6 makes you feel angry.
7 shows little thought or judges things badly.
8 likes being with people.
9 is relaxed and not easily upset.
10 is easily upset by what people say and do.
11 you can trust.
12 always thinks of how to make other people happy.

2 Choose the correct answer.

1 Susie is such a *sensible / sensitive* girl. She cares too much about what people think.
2 Ben's got loads of friends. He's very *loyal / sociable.*
3 Jake was very *sensible / sensitive* and went to bed early the night before his test.
4 My friend is *annoying / reliable* because he keeps changing the date of his party.
5 Yesterday we laughed so much about little things – we were really *silly / talented.*
6 My test is tomorrow and I feel *anxious / reliable* because I haven't studied.
7 Duncan is so *anxious / thoughtful* – he's always very kind to other people.
8 Frank is a *loyal / reliable* student – he always does his homework on time.

3 Choose a word from the box to describe each teen.

anxious	annoying	easygoing	jealous
loyal	reliable	sensible	sensitive
silly	sociable	talented	thoughtful

I make sure I do something when I say I'll do it.
1 ....
I sometimes feel unhappy and angry if someone has something I want.
2 ....
I'm worried about the maths test tomorrow – I haven't done enough work.
3 ....
I love hanging out with friends and being with people.
4 ....
I really don't mind which film we see – both are probably good.
5 ....
I get upset very easily by things people do or say to me.
6 ....
I'm lucky because it isn't hard for me to draw really great pictures of people.
7 ....
I never say anything bad about friends to other people and I always keep people's secrets.
8 ....

1 Read the title of the article. What do you think the four friends like about their BFF (best friend forever)?

2 Now read the article quickly. Are your ideas there?

MY BEST FRIEND FOREVER

KENNEDY

'Ruth's a real friend. We don't spend all our time together, but she's there when I need her and she's very loyal. Last term, a girl in my class posted unpleasant things about me on my social media page. Some people believed them and were unkind to me. Ruth wasn't. She wasn't afraid of telling everyone that what the girl said wasn't true. She told me to unfriend the girl and I did. Ruth and I like chatting about things we're interested in doing. We both love dancing and listening to music. Sometimes Ruth comes on holiday with me and my family – that's fun!'

CHRIS

'My best mate is Angelo. He's from Italy and when he first arrived here, he was anxious about not being able to speak English very well. Some people laughed at the way he spoke, which I didn't think was very kind, so I helped him with his English after school and we became friends. We like playing football and going swimming in the river. He's a really thoughtful guy. When he goes back to visit family in Italy, he always brings me a present when he returns – usually something to eat because he knows I'm really keen on Italian food!'

OLIVIA

'For me, a true friend is someone who shows their friendship rather than just tells you they're your friend but then doesn't act that way. I'll give you an example: in art class one day, I drew a silly picture of my teacher. It wasn't unkind. I just really like drawing people and making funny pictures. Anyway, it dropped out of my bag and the teacher found it and was unhappy about it. My friend Jenny went to the head teacher's office and said she drew it because I was already in trouble for something else! That probably wasn't very sensible, but Jenny was good to me that day and I'll never forget it.'

ADAM

'Hanging out with Jake's great fun. We're both crazy about gaming, so we spend a lot of time trying to win! Jake's really good at games, but I don't mind losing, because we always have a great time. He's a really talented skateboarder, too – he's amazing to watch. He's teaching me a few tricks at the moment. I don't feel very confident yet, but he's really kind and patient. I'll never be as good as he is at skateboarding, but he's a brilliant teacher!'

3 Read the sentences below. Read the article again and decide if each sentence is correct or incorrect. Write C for correct or I for incorrect.

1 Kennedy did something kind for her friend Ruth at school.

2 Ruth wasn't scared of people in her class.

3 Angelo likes to do nice things for Chris.

4 Olivia's friend Jenny did something wrong.

5 Olivia felt that Jenny was cruel for talking to the head teacher.

6 Adam doesn't think it's a problem when Jake wins games.

4 Match the highlighted words in the article to the meanings.

1 a friend

2 not nice or enjoyable

3 behave

4 part of the school year

5 can wait without feeling angry

1 Complete the sentences with the *-ing* form of the verb in brackets.

1 The teacher doesn't mind _____ (describe) grammar rules again.

2 My friend Nathan enjoys _____ (run) early in the morning with his dad.

3 I can't stand _____ (do) homework at the weekend.

4 _____ (go) on holiday is good for you.

5 I think Mum's tired of _____ (clean) my bedroom for me.

6 Yvonne likes _____ (meet) new people because she's very sociable.

7 _____ (learn) new things helps our brains stay young and healthy.

8 Sally always stays on the beach when we go to the seaside because she hates _____ (swim) in the sea.

2 Write sentences. Use the correct form of the verbs.

0 Julia / love / make / a big breakfast for her parents.
Julia loves making a big breakfast for her parents.

1 Mikey / can't stand / go / food shopping.

2 Ella / not really like / watch / horror films.

3 Jade / enjoy / send videos / to her friends.

4 Morgan / like / play / basketball / with his friends after school.

5 Philippa / not mind / stay / home alone.

6 Harry / hate / listen to / rock and pop music.

7 Maria / tired of / live / on her own.

8 Jordan / doesn't enjoy / shop / with his sisters.

3 Match the adjectives to the prepositions.

1 afraid _____   **a** on
2 good _____   **b** at
3 keen _____   **c** in
4 crazy _____   **d** about
5 interested _____ **e** of

4 Complete the text with a preposition from A and a verb from B. Use the *-ing* form of the verb.

A about	at	in	of	on
B catch	do	have	play	walk

My friends and I are interested ¹ _____ the same things. We are all really crazy ² _____ the same sports. We're all keen ³ _____ a game of basketball together whenever we can – even the ones who aren't very good ⁴ _____ the ball. Sometimes we play for hours and finish very late! Then, Mum collects me because she knows I'm afraid ⁵ _____ home in the dark on my own.

5 Correct the mistakes in these sentences or put a tick (✓) by any you think are correct.

1 Write letters is a very old-fashioned thing to do now.

2 I like see my friends at the weekends.

3 I'm quite good at making new friends.

4 We enjoy spend time together because it's fun.

5 We like doing homework or study together.

6 What do you like doing with your friends?

1 Write the negative form of the verb or adjective in brackets to complete the sentences.

1 I thought our teacher was _____ when he gave us extra homework. (kind)

2 This room smells _____. Let's open the window. (pleasant)

3 You were _____ getting that question in the quiz – it was hard. (lucky)

4 I _____ with you: most football players earn too much money. (agree)

5 Zak suddenly _____ from the party. (appear)

6 This programme is so _____ Let's watch something else. (interesting)

7 Maria looked quite _____ this morning. What's wrong? (happy)

8 I really _____ this kind of TV programme. Everyone shouts in them! (like)

9 Benjy _____ Eva on social media because she isn't nice to him. (friend)

2 Complete the conversations with one of these verbs or adjectives, or its negative form. There are two words which you don't need to use.

agree	appear	happy	friend
interesting	kind	like	lucky

1 A: I don't think we have enough homework – we need more at the weekend.
 B: I _____ with you! We've got too much!

2 A: I loved reading this book.
 B: Me too! It was really _____ and I learned a lot.

3 A: I love my friends.
 B: Same here! We're so _____ to have them.

4 A: Do you like geography?
 B: No, I really _____ it. It's difficult and I don't understand it.

5 A: Do you know what's wrong with Maggie? She's very quiet today.
 B: Well, I know she's _____ but I don't know why.

6 A: Did you meet my friend Nick?
 B: Yes, he's lovely and he said some really _____ things about you.

1 You will hear an announcement about writing an article for a website. Tick (✓) the topics you think the announcement will include.

what the article should be about
where people can read the article
how many words the article should be
examples of what to include
when the article should be finished

 **2** Listen and check your answers.

✓ PREPARE FOR THE EXAM

Listening Part 3

3 Listen again. For each question, write the correct answer in the gap. Write one or two words, or a number or a date or a time.

Write an article about friendship

The article should be about how
[1] _____ is changing people's friendships.

Include reasons for reading friends'
[2] _____ on their own web pages.

Write about the [3] _____ of a good friend you have.

Explain a [4] _____ where an online or 'real' friend gave their help.

Talk about the different kinds of
[5] _____ you have with friends.

Your article should not be longer than
[6] _____ words.

✓ EXAM TIPS

- Look at the six gaps in the notes before you listen.
- Consider possible answers, but do not write them in the gaps before listening.

3 FUN AND GAMES

VOCABULARY   Sports phrases

1 Write the letters in the correct order to make verbs.

0	neetr	*enter a competition/tournament*
1	vieg	
2	onji	
3	sism	
4	teab	
5	soel	
6	niw	
7	ahev	
8	csoer	

2 Add words from the box to complete the phrases in Exercise 1, as in the example.

> a club/gym ~~a competition/tournament~~
> a go at something   a goal/point
> a game/match   a prize/medal/game/match
> (someone) the chance   the opportunity
> the other team

3 Chose the correct answer.

1 Jake *entered / gave* a competition.
2 Maria's team *scored / won* a goal.
3 This year I *missed / gave* the opportunity to go scuba diving. What a pity!
4 The captain *joined / gave* me the chance to play in goal.
5 The Jones family have *had / joined* a gym because they want to get fit.
6 David is sad because his team *lost / entered* the match.
7 During our activity week at school, you can *have / give* a go at lots of different sports.
8 At the end of the tournament, I *won / join* a prize – I came first!
9 We *won / beat* the other team 4–0!

4 Complete the sentences with verbs and nouns from Exercises 1 and 2.

1 Sam really wants to _____ – then he can wear it round his neck!
2 My dad wants to _____ ! He's excited about getting fit.
3 Oh no! We're going to _____. The other team are much better.
4 Do you want to _____ surfing? You can borrow my board if you like.

5 Mark and his football team are raising money for their sports club. Here are some things they are doing. Use the prompts to write complete sentences. Use the present simple.

1 In our football team / everyone / give some money / when we score / goal

2 Everyone who / enter / tournament / next week / have to pay / €5.00

3 Every time / we / have / go / at a new sport / we / give / some money to the sports club

4 When we / win / a match / the other team / give / money / to our club

1 Read the title of the article. What do you think a sports volunteer does? Read the text quickly and check your ideas.

My experience as a
SPORTS
VOLUNTEER

by Sandie Jones

I volunteer for a netball organisation – netball's a bit like basketball but usually played by women. I've never actually done it – it was offered as a sport at school, but I chose football, instead. I rarely bother to turn the TV on for sports matches, as I don't have a lot of time – I prefer to be out at the weekends and being a volunteer is a great way to do that. I thought it would be interesting to know what netball is.

I do various jobs when I'm volunteering. Matches usually take place on Saturdays, so I arrive early to help check that the court is free of stones or rubbish. Then I prepare drinks and snacks for the players before collecting tickets when spectators start to arrive. There's nothing particularly hard to do, though sometimes I wouldn't mind having a bit more of a challenge – maybe to help sort out the matches themselves, like which teams are playing and when. I think I'd be good at that, but I'm not complaining – I enjoy everything I do!

The matches are great fun and I love watching people who are so good at what they do. I always go home feeling amazed. It doesn't matter to me which team wins, which might sound like a strange thing to say, but the best team always wins on the day and you can't argue with that, even if the players are unhappy about losing. Spectators do look upset sometimes when their team doesn't win, but you can understand that. You'd expect the players to behave well, but sometimes they show that they're annoyed, and that's a pity, because they're all nice people, really.

I'd encourage other people to be a volunteer. It's probably more interesting if you like the sport involved, but it doesn't matter because you'll learn a lot about yourself and other people, and make great friends. This isn't something you can only do if you want to get a job in sport. It's just good fun and you won't have to do anything you don't want to. It's just nice to spend time with people from your town, outside school or college!

PREPARE FOR THE EXAM

Reading Part 3

2 Read the article and questions below. For each question, choose A, B, C or D.

1 Sandie was keen to help with a sport she
  A likes watching.
  B was good at herself.
  C wanted to find out about.
  D had never had the chance to try.

2 What does Sandie say about the jobs she does as a volunteer?
  A She finds some of them challenging.
  B She doesn't enjoy doing some of them.
  C She'd like to do a greater variety of jobs.
  D She'd like to try using her skills a different way.

3 How does Sandie feel at the end of matches?
  A excited by the skills she has seen
  B disappointed when her team loses
  C surprised by how the spectators behave
  D impressed by the attitude of the players

4 Why does Sandie recommend becoming a volunteer?
  A Volunteers learn many new skills.
  B It can help volunteers get jobs in sport.
  C It provides the chance to meet new people.
  D Volunteers give something back to the community.

5 What advert would Sandie write to find new volunteers?
  A I'm looking for volunteers to help me at the netball club which I run. Having some knowledge of netball is necessary.
  B Come and be a volunteer! You only need to give a couple of hours a week and help local sports events go well.
  C Do you want to be a sports volunteer for a well-known club? If so, send me an email with details of your previous experience.
  D Do you enjoy playing netball? You could be the perfect volunteer for our club. You'll even get the chance to play in matches!

EXAM TIPS

• Read the whole text first for meaning.
• Read the questions and the options carefully before choosing your answer.

1 Use the words to make sentences in the present simple or present continuous tense.

0 I / have / lots of fun!
I'm having lots of fun!

1 Nancy / run / the same route / every morning

2 We / do / our homework / for tomorrow

3 I / stay / with my sister / for the weekend

4 All cameras / work / in a similar way / I / think

5 I / want / learn / to play American football

2 Are the <u>underlined</u> verbs in these sentences correct (C) or incorrect (I)? Correct them if necessary.

1 <u>I'm talking</u> to my friends on Facebook at the moment.
2 Dad <u>is playing</u> golf with his friends every Saturday morning.
3 By ten o'clock most evenings, <u>I'm feeling</u> tired and ready for bed.
4 Tess <u>is having</u> a picnic with her friend Jenny tomorrow.
5 Does anyone know how this app <u>is working</u>?
6 Mum never <u>gets</u> the train to work – she says it's too slow!
7 The Earth <u>is going round</u> the Sun.

3 Complete the conversation with the correct form of the verbs in the box.

do	fix	go	have	install
(not) know	meet	want	(not) work	

Anna: What ¹ _____ at the moment, Fred?
Fred: Oh, you know, things. Nothing special really, although I ² _____ Martin in town at three. I always ³ _____ into town with him on Saturday afternoons. Why do you want to know?
Anna: Well, my other phone ⁴ _____ properly and I ⁵ _____ you to look at it.
Fred: Oh, OK, but I ⁶ _____ much about phones.
Anna: But you ⁷ _____ phones, don't you? Dad said you're fixing his phone at the moment!
Fred: No, I ⁸ _____ a program – it's different.
Anna: Oh, OK. I'll think of something. See you at home later – we ⁹ _____ pancakes for dinner! Don't be late!

4 Choose the correct sentence in each pair.

👁 **1 a** I'm thinking the gym opens at nine o'clock, if you are wanting to come.
   b I think the gym opens at nine o'clock, if you want to come.

2 a Every Friday and Saturday we are having a basketball lesson.
   b Every Friday and Saturday we have a basketball lesson.

3 a We play football very often and in the past we were in the same football club.
   b We're playing football very often and in the past we were in the same football club.

4 a I'm going to the pool this evening for a swim.
   b I go to the pool this evening for a swim.

1 Add the correct suffix, -ist, -er, or -or to the ends of these words and remember to make any necessary spelling changes.

1 John is an excellent climb _____. He's planning to go up Everest soon!
2 My brother's an Olympic canoe _____.
3 We won the match on Sunday – the spectat _____ s went crazy!
4 My friend Verity wants to be a world champion surf _____.
5 Isn't your sister a football _____? I think I saw her play on Saturday.
6 My grandfather was a sail _____ all his life. He travelled all over the world.
7 Who do you think the win _____ s of this year's championship will be?
8 I'm not a very good swim _____ because I didn't have lessons when I was young.

2 Complete each sentence with a word from the box. Add a suffix if required and remember to make any necessary spelling changes.

cycle	compete	final
lose	medal	support

1 Melanie is a silver _____ in gymnastics.
2 Shall we _____ into town and have lunch?
3 Will you _____ in the tournament next month?
4 Our team's _____ are brilliant. They come to watch every match!
5 Will all _____ please take their starting positions now.
6 I really hope we don't _____ this match – we're doing really badly at the moment.

1 An organisation called International Wheelchair and Amputee Sports Federation (IWAS) holds competitions in the following sports. Do you know what they are?

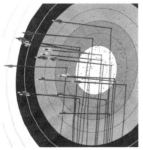

2 Match the pictures in Exercise 1 with the activities in the box.

archery   powerlifting   rugby
shooting   table tennis   volleyball

3 Read a post on a sports club website and the comment. Answer the question.

IWASYouth

The IWASYouth Games includes competitions in sports including athletics, swimming, table tennis, rugby and volleyball. We'd like to start up a new sports club for young people with disabilities so they can train to compete in similar events. Which sports do you think we should offer?

What does the sports club want to do?

4 Read the comment in reply to the post. Answer the question.

Comments

JULIA

There are a lot of sports which people with disabilities can do. For example, there's wheelchair racing and racing for people who use blades. You can play lots of team sports in wheelchairs, too, like football or basketball. These would be good things to offer at our sports club because they aren't too expensive and we already have the facilities.

Why does Julia think racing and team sports would be good things to offer at the club?

5 Read Julia's comment again. Find two phrases which she uses to make suggestions or recommendations. Can you think of other ways to make suggestions or recommendations?

6 Now write your own reply to the post.

Decide what to say in your reply.

Use phrases for making suggestions or recommendations.

Write about 100 words.

4 EXTREME WEATHER

1 Write the words from the box under the pictures.

> earthquake   flood   lightning   snowstorm   tornado

1 _____

2 _____

3 _____

4 _____

5 _____

2 Complete the sentences with the correct form of the verbs below.

> blow   fall   pour   rise   shake

1 The wind is _____ so hard. I think the roof might come off our house!
2 I think there was an earthquake yesterday because the ground _____ for a few seconds.
3 The rain _____ for hours yesterday. I thought there might be a flood.
4 The big tree in our garden _____ down in the winter storms.
5 The level of the water in the river always _____ when it rains a lot.

3 Complete the sentences with the correct form of the words in Exercises 1 and 2.

1 I hate it when there's a _____ – there's water everywhere.
2 The _____ was like something out of a film – the wind was lifting everything up.
3 Oh look! That girl's hat is going to _____ away.
4 My grandfather loves watching the _____ in the sky during a storm.
5 Have you got an umbrella? It's going to _____ with rain later today.
6 Look at this line. It shows how high the river can _____ when it rains a lot.

4 Choose the correct word to complete the sentences.

1 There was a terrible *flood / lightening* last year. The whole village was under water.
2 Have you ever seen a *tornado / flood* moving across the desert? It's amazing how fast they can go.
3 The wind's *pouring / blowing* quite strongly. I don't think we should go climbing today.
4 The level of the river *rose / poured* quickly because it was raining so hard.
5 Wow! That *lightning / tornado* during the storm last night was amazing! I could see the whole street even though it was dark.
6 It's *blowing / pouring* with rain. Let's stay in and watch a film.

1 Read the article quickly, ignoring the gaps. Which text message do you think the girl in paragraph 3 sent her friend the next day?

> **1** Wow! That was a crazy day yesterday!

> **2** The forecast predicted a sunny day. I wanted to swim.

> **3** Grandma and I found some amazing plants for sale.

2 Look at the sentences with gaps in the article. What kind of word is missing from each sentence: a verb or an adjective?

KAPITI MINI TORNADO

At about 2 pm yesterday, high winds destroyed houses and trees as bad weather hit the Kapiti coast in New Zealand.

The mini tornado was a frightening event that started with rain and wind. The wind blew ¹_____, the sky went a strange colour and huge balls of ice ²_____ from the sky. This ³_____ a lot of cars and buildings, and the wind began to ⁴_____ the roofs off the houses.

One girl, whose grandfather is the owner of a shop selling things for the garden, was helping her grandmother to ⁵_____ plants back inside the main building when it was hit by the tornado. Fortunately, she was not hurt, though she was very scared by what happened.

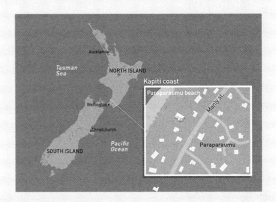

The whole area was ⁶_____ with no power for a long time, and many buildings needed repairs afterwards.

Reading Part 5

3 Read the article and choose the correct answer.

	A	**B**	**C**	**D**
1	heavier	thicker	harder	darker
2	pulled	broke	passed	fell
3	damaged	hurt	injured	lost
4	hold	lift	climb	rise
5	turn	stay	move	keep
6	left	remained	held	dropped

4 Match the highlighted words and phrases in the article to the meanings.

1 damaged so much that it does not exist or cannot be used
2 strong
3 something you do to fix something that is broken or damaged
4 making you feel nervous or afraid

- Read the text through to get a good idea of what it is about.
- Look at the four options for each gap and think about which word fits best.

1 Complete the sentences with the verbs in the past simple tense.

1 The weather forecast _____ (not be) very good, so we decided not to go to the beach.
2 The wind _____ (blow) so hard that I could hardly walk down the street!
3 The storm was so violent that it _____ (damage) buildings and cars all over the town.
4 The winter floods _____ (destroy) many homes in the region.
5 The number of bush fires _____ (rise) to 60,000 last year.
6 The high winds _____ (create) a powerful tornado that raced across the land.
7 Fortunately, the lightning _____ (not hit) the skyscraper.
8 The rain _____ (fall) so heavily that the street turned into a river!

2 Complete the conversation with verbs from the box. Use the present simple or past simple form.

buy	do	help	know	not play
not think		want	work	

Mike: What ¹ _____ you _____ last weekend?
Jack: Nothing much. I went to my grandparents'. They ² _____ a new computer.
Mike: Oh, ³ _____ you _____ them to set it up?
Jack: Not really. Granddad ⁴ _____ quite a lot about computers.
Mike: Oh, yes. He ⁵ _____ in computers, didn't he?
Jack: Yes, he did. He ⁶ _____ a more powerful computer to surf and play games on, so that's why they got a new one.
Mike: Wow! My grandparents ⁷ _____ computer games. I ⁸ _____ they're interested.
Jack: Well, mine are! Sometimes I play with them!

3 Write questions in the past simple tense for these answers.

0 *What time did you get up this morning?*
I got up at about 7.30.
1 _____
Yes, I did. I had some toast and jam.
2 _____
I came to school by car this morning – Dad brought me.
3 _____
Yes, but I was nearly late because the roads were very busy.
4 _____
I went to my classroom and said hello to everyone.

4 Write the words in the correct order to make sentences about what Adrian did when he was younger.

1 to / live / used / Adrian / Canada / in
2 to / He / used / a pair of / have / snow boots
3 walk / to / He / didn't / school / to / use
4 in his classes / used / French / speak / to / He
5 to / He / go / used / on holiday / to / the lakes
6 go / to / use / skiing / He / in winter / didn't
7 to / used / a lot of / wear / He / clothes / warm
8 dream / to / the snow! / He / used / about

5 What did Julia use to do when she was a young girl? Write sentences.

1	do boxing	✓
2	eat green vegetables	✗
3	play with a toy train set	✓
4	climb trees	✓
5	speak English	✗
6	go to bed early	✓
7	have lots of homework	✗
8	play computer games	✗

6 Correct the mistakes in these sentences or put a tick (✓) by any you think are correct.

1 I meet her at school when I was nine years old.
2 I go to the restaurant last Saturday with my friend.
3 It was hard work, but it was worth it.
4 We use to study together.
5 We used to went biking a lot together, but we don't see each other often now.
6 We weren't classmates, but we used to talk a lot after lessons.

1 Choose the correct words to complete the text.

There used to be a great restaurant just outside our village, but it isn't there anymore because of the extreme weather we had this summer. First, there was a huge storm and the wind blew all the outside tables and chairs ¹ *away / up*. A beautiful old tree in the restaurant garden fell ² *down / away*, too. The rain was awful, but when the sun came ³ *down / out* later, everywhere became very dry and it didn't rain again for weeks. This led to forest fires, and the restaurant burnt ⁴ *away / down* because firefighters didn't arrive in time to put it ⁵ *away / out*. The damage was cleared ⁶ *down / up*, and the owners hope to build a new restaurant in the same place.

2 Complete the sentences with the correct form of the phrasal verbs in the box.

blow away	burn down	clear up
come out	fall down	put out

1 Do you remember that huge pine tree in our garden? Well, it .... during the storm last night.
2 Many houses .... during the recent forest fires.
3 It's too windy to work outside – all our papers will ....
4 Everyone got together and .... after the flood. There was mud everywhere.
5 Jonas helped the firefighters to .... the fire.
6 As we walked home, the sun .... at last.

LISTENING

1 Where can you find out about what to do in extreme weather conditions?

1 the internet ☐
2 books ☐
3 school ☐
4 ask people (who?) ☐
5 your own ideas ☐

 ## PREPARE FOR THE EXAM

Listening Part 4

2 You will hear an interview with a girl called Lacey Anderson, who writes a blog about the weather. For each question, choose the correct answer.

1 Why did Lacey decide to write a blog about the weather?
  A It seemed like a good way to help her become a TV weather presenter.
  B She enjoyed sharing her photos of extreme weather conditions online.
  C There was little information available about weather in her area.
2 What does Lacey think people like about her blog?
  A They can follow links to other websites about weather.
  B They can upload information about weather in their area.
  C They can ask questions about future weather events.
3 When asked about the effects of her blog on readers, Lacey says she feels
  A surprised that they take notice of what she suggests.
  B pleased that they offer advice based on their experiences.
  C excited that they encourage other people to read her blog.
4 Lacey says that her local weather centre has
  A given her information that she couldn't find anywhere else.
  B saved her a lot of time and effort.
  C provided pictures free of charge.
5 Lacey's parents decided to get involved in her blog when
  A they got jobs as firefighters.
  B Lacey asked them to write an article about forest fires.
  C they learned about how a particular fire started.
6 What does Lacey say about the organisations which support her blog?
  A Her school allows her to take time out of class to write her blog.
  B The local newspaper regularly prints positive reviews of her blog.
  C A shop in the area gave her some products to sell through her blog.

EXAM TIPS

- Read the questions and all three options before you listen.
- The questions follow the order of information in the recording and show you what information to listen for.

5 YOU MADE IT!

1 Match the verbs to their meanings.

1 create	....	**a** make or repair clothes by joining cloth using a needle and thread
2 customise	....	**b** repair something that is broken or not working properly
3 design	....	**c** change something to make it suitable for a particular person or purpose
4 decorate	....	**d** make something that has never existed before
5 sew	....	**e** draw or plan
6 fix	....	**f** repair clothes that are broken or torn
7 rebuild	....	**g** add attractive things to something
8 recycle	....	**h** collect used paper, glass, plastic and other things and use them again
9 mend	....	**i** build again

2 Choose the correct answer for each sentence.

1 I'm going to .... a new type of pocket to go inside trousers!
   a design   **b** rebuild   **c** mend
2 Oh, no! I've just broken my phone. I'd better take it back to the shop and see if they can .... it.
   a create   **b** customise   **c** fix
3 One of my friends always .... her school bags with pictures of her favourite actor.
   a fixes   **b** rebuilds   **c** decorates
4 These little leather flowers are so pretty. I'm going to .... a couple of them onto my new jacket.
   a create   **b** sew   **c** decorate
5 My dad's an architect and he's .... a completely new type of building.
   a decorated   **b** recycled   **c** designed
6 My bike's very old and broken now, but I won't throw it away; I'll .... it instead.
   a recycle   **b** design   **c** create

3 Complete the sentences with the verbs in the correct form. There is one verb in each set that you do not need.

1 customise   decorate   design
    fix   sew

A: This bag is so boring. I'd like to ....
it with something – like these red hearts, perhaps.
B: Why don't you put your name on it and
.... it completely?
A: Good idea! No one else will have one like it! I'll
.... some cool letters to put on it.
B: Good idea! And I'll .... them on the
bag for you.

2 design   fix   mend   recycle   sew

A: Your bike isn't working again – you're going to
have to .... it.
B: Oh, not again. Look at it! I don't know who
.... this type of bike, but it's not
very good.
A: Why don't you just .... it and buy
yourself a new one?
B: I think I'll .... it one more time and
save up for a new one.

3 create   decorate   rebuild   recycle   sew

A: I think that we can use this material again, you
know, ... it.
B: Yes, we can .... something
completely new!
A: Like a dress, maybe? I can .... the
different pieces of material together.
B: OK, and I could .... the pockets with
little flowers in a pattern or something.

4 customise   design   mend
    rebuild   recycle

A: That building's beautiful – that glass wall looks
so amazing.
Who .... it?
B: No idea, but it looks like they are ....
part of it. Look, there's some stone and other
things over there.
A: No, they haven't finished building it yet! And look!
They're .... it by sticking metal letters
all over the walls. Maybe it's the company name…
B: Oh, yeah! It looks like they're using
.... materials, too – they're creating
the letters from old bike parts!

1 You are going to read an article about an artist called Haroshi. Read the article quickly. What is unusual about Haroshi's art?

Reading Part 4

2 Five sentences have been removed from the article. For each question, choose the correct answer. There are three extra sentences which you do not need to use.

   A Other skateboarders threw theirs away when this happened, but Haroshi didn't because they were important to him.

   B Using this material isn't the only interesting thing about his work, though.

   C When he stopped skateboarding, he needed to find a new way to fill his time.

   D While he was doing this, he realised that he could create something new from something old.

   E Haroshi took this idea and does something similar in his own work.

   F He saw these sculptures and decided to do something completely different.

   G Haroshi had no formal training in art, and each piece of work took a very long time because of this.

   H He asked their opinions about what he was doing and they gave him their old skateboards, too.

EXAM TIPS

- If you don't understand some of the words in the text, don't worry: just read for the general meaning.
- Read the sentences before and after each gap carefully before you choose your answer.

3 Match the highlighted words and phrases in the article to the meanings.

   1 person
   2 be different from each other
   3 in the end, especially after a long time
   4 joined with glue
   5 very interested or enthusiastic

Haroshi's skateboard
Sculptures

Japanese artist, Haroshi, creates amazing sculptures from old skateboards.

Haroshi began skateboarding when he was 15 years old and loved it. He went every day and used many skateboards, each of which eventually broke from being used so much. ¹_____ Over time, he built up a large collection of them. While he was doing so, he learned about different types of skateboard, which not only vary in size and shape but can be built in different ways, too. By the time he was 25, Haroshi had an enormous number of old skateboards.

Keen to do something with them, Haroshi started to cut them up. As he was doing so, he noticed interesting patterns in the wood. He cut up more boards and stuck them on top of each other. ²_____ The first thing he produced from the old wood was a piece of jewellery, but he later became known for his huge 3D sculptures. His ideas came from skateboarding culture, ranging from skateboarding cats to cool trainers, and a variety of other everyday subjects. ³_____. What this showed was that he had a huge amount of natural talent and was keen to show his work to the world.

Haroshi's work has been seen in several exhibitions, where everything from an enormous bird to a figure of a man in pain have been on display. One sculpture, called *Ordinary life*, looks like a broken leg – a reality of skateboarding – and it is incredible to think that Haroshi designs and creates each sculpture from old wood. ⁴_____
In the twelfth century, a Japanese sculptor called Unkei placed a glass ball in each of his sculptures, to show that each piece had a heart. ⁵_____
Inside each of his sculptures is a piece of broken skateboard. This, Haroshi believes, is what gives his sculptures life.

 **GRAMMAR** Past simple and continuous

1 **Choose the correct form of the verb.**

As I [1] *was cycling / cycled* home from school yesterday, I was feeling pleased because I [2] *wasn't having / didn't have* any homework. I thought about what I would do that evening instead. I was so busy [3] *tried / trying* to decide how to spend my free time that I [4] *missed / was missing* the end of my road and cycled twenty minutes before I [5] *was realising / realised* ! I stopped near my friend's house, so I [6] *went / was going* to visit him and we spent the evening playing computer games.

2 **Complete the sentences with the verbs in the past continuous or past simple.**

1 When I was young, I _____ (want) to be a pilot.
2 Maggie _____ (text) a friend when her mother _____ (call) her for dinner.
3 What _____ you _____ (do) last night? I called you but there was no answer. I _____ (watch) TV with my family. I didn't hear my phone.
4 Rick _____ (take) my photo and _____ (upload) it to Facebook.
5 No one really _____ (understand) what they had to do for the homework project, so they asked the teacher.
6 I last _____ (see) my cousin when she _____ (visit) us two years ago.
7 Monique _____ (walk) home from school when her mum _____ (drive) past her.
8 Jules _____ (win) the competition and we _____ (hear) the news last night.

3 **Complete the text with the verbs in the box in the correct form. Two of the verbs should be in the negative form.**

be	can	chat	decide	manage
receive	ring	send	work	

Yesterday my friends and I [1] _____ during the morning break when Jake [2] _____ a text from our friend Aysha. She was sick and told us that she [3] _____ come to school for the rest of the week. So we [4] _____ to send her a photo of us all with a 'Get well soon' message. Unfortunately, my phone [5] _____ very well and the picture wasn't clear. It [6] _____ a bit annoying but we finally [7] _____ to take a good picture. As we [8] _____ it, the school bell [9] _____ to tell us that break was over. Perfect timing!

4 **Read the conversation and complete the questions below.**

Sam: What did you do in art last week?
Toby: We talked about our end-of-year project.
Sam: Oh, yeah? I heard there was a problem or something.
Toby: Well, the teacher left the room for a minute and we all started talking. Sarah was finishing her work while we were chatting, and as she was mixing her paints, suddenly there was a loud clap of thunder. It made us all jump and Sarah spilled her paint everywhere. We were all laughing when the teacher came back into the room.
Sam: Uh oh!
Toby: Well, it was fine because we explained what had happened, but I don't think Sarah will be able to hand in that painting for her end-of-year project now!

0 *What did the students talk about in art last week?*
The end-of-year project.
1 What _____ ?
Finishing her work.
2 What _____ ?
A loud clap of thunder.
3 What _____ ?
She spilled her paints.
4 Who _____ ?
The teacher.
5 Why _____ ?
Because they explained what had happened to her.

5 **Correct the mistakes in these sentences or put a tick (✓) by any you think are correct.**

1 Last year, I was going to a place in Mexico named Mazatlán. It was amazing.

2 I am talking to a friend, when Joe came up to speak to me.

3 Last weekend was fantastic and I had a lot of fun.

4 The music was so good, that I was dancing all night!

5 When we saw our friends in the park they played football.

1 Choose the correct adverb.

We had our maths test yesterday. [1] *First / Later*, we walked into the classroom and [2] *suddenly / then* we sat down. [3] *First / Next*, the teacher gave us our test papers and we were about to start the test but [4] *suddenly / finally*, there was a huge bang outside and fireworks filled the sky! Our teacher thought that it was a party somewhere nearby. [5] *Finally / Next*, when it went quiet again, we began our test. [6] *Later / First*, we discovered that a fire had started in a fireworks factory across town!

2 Complete the email with the adverbs in the box.

finally	first	later	next
suddenly	then		

Hi Megan,
You didn't miss a lot in art today.
[1] _____, we had to choose what we wanted to draw. Mr Jenkins had brought some different objects and we had to choose one each. [2] _____, he asked us to decide whether we wanted to use either pencil or charcoal to draw it, and [3] _____ we collected some paper before starting our work. [4] _____, the fire alarm rang and we all had to go and stand outside. We were there for a long time. [5] _____, we went back into the art class, but there were only five minutes of the lesson left, so Mr Jenkins said we should finish the work [6] _____. We'll probably do it in our next class, so you'll be able to do it, too!
Hope you get better soon,
Stevie

1 Read a student's answer to a Writing Part 2 task (story) and answer the questions.

Jennifer didn't really like the sweater her sister had bought her for her birthday. What was she going to do? She didn't want to wear it, but if she didn't, her sister would be upset and ask her why.

Jennifer sat and thought about her problem for a while. Suddenly, she had an idea. 'I know, I'll customise it!' she decided, and got out her sewing box.

1 Does the story have a good beginning, middle and ending?
2 How would you end the story? Make some notes, then compare your ideas with a partner.

_____
_____
_____

3 Which of these endings to the story do you think is better? Why?
a She looked into her box and found some old bits of material and cut them into star shapes. She sewed them onto the sweater in an interesting pattern. 'Wow! I love that design!' said her sister. Jennifer was pleased because now they were both happy.
b She looked for interesting things she could put on the sweater and found some interesting pieces of material. 'I'll sew these on,' she thought. When she finished, Jennifer was really happy with her sweater and put it on.

✅ PREPARE FOR THE EXAM

Writing Part 2 (A story)

2 Write a story

Your English teacher has asked you to write a story.
Your story should begin with this sentence:
Jed really wanted to win the art competition at school.
Write your **story** in about **100** words.

✅ EXAM TIPS
- Read the sentence you must use carefully and think about how your story will develop.
- Make a few notes about the beginning, middle and end of your story. Try to make it interesting!

6 TAKE CARE OF YOURSELF

VOCABULARY Health verbs

1 Complete the crossword, using the clues on the right.

[crossword grid with numbered squares 1–8]

1 force air out of your body, often when you have a cold
2 hurt a person or part of your body
3 open your mouth and take air in because you are tired or bored
4 have a pain which is continuous and isn't very nice
5 be hurt by fire or heat
6 lose blood
7 become well again after being ill
8 hurt yourself on a sharp object and produce blood

2 Write the letters in the correct order to make words and complete the sentences.

1 wobl
If you've got a cold, _____ your nose into a tissue and throw it away.

2 tbearhe
I can't _____ through my nose at the moment because I've got flu.

3 tesab
Your heart often _____ faster when you are not very well.

4 nbru
Be careful not to _____ yourself on the cooker!

5 lbnki
My eyes hurt when I _____. I don't know what's wrong with them.

6 heac
Sorry, but I won't be at work today because I've got a painful _____ in my back.

7 rcveore
You need time to _____ after a big operation.

8 juinerd
The footballer has _____ himself again and can't play in today's match.

9 gohcu
I've got a horrible _____ at the moment and my chest really hurts.

10 gbldieen
Your finger's _____! What have you done to it?

3 Complete the article with the correct form of the verbs in the box. You do not need to use all the words.

ache	beat	burn	bleed
blink	blow	breathe	cough
cut	injure	recover	yawn

HEALTH MATTERS:

Taking care of your head

This week in Health Matters, we're taking a look at the head. One very common thing that many of you complain about is an ¹ _____ head and itchy eyes, especially when you're using the computer. To reduce these problems, try to spend less time in front of the screen and when you're working, remember to ² _____ often and allow your eyes to rest. If you start ³ _____, that's a warning that you're getting tired, so take a break!

Playing sport means there is always a chance that you will ⁴ _____ yourself. Wear a helmet if you can, and if you do fall or bang your head, make sure you give yourself time to ⁵ _____ before going back on the field.

What should you do if your nose is ⁶ _____? Put your head forward and hold the top of your nose where it's narrow. Stay like this until it stops and if it doesn't stop, see a doctor as soon as you can.

And finally, colds. These can make you feel pretty bad, especially when you can't stop ⁷ _____ and your nose is so blocked that you can't ⁸ _____ very well. When you've got a cold, get some medicine from the pharmacy, take time off and get some rest.

Next week's article is all about the neck. See you then!

1 Read about the effects of drinking caffeine and choose the best title for the article.

1 You are what you eat!   **2** Health drinks   **3** Fast and fizzy

If your heart starts beating quickly after you've had a can of cola or other fizzy drink, then you should listen carefully to what your body's trying to tell you. Many fizzy drinks contain caffeine, like coffee does, and this is what wakes you up and gives you energy. It can also make you breathe more quickly and even affect your sleep, as well as raise your blood pressure, which could put you at risk of a heart attack or other medical condition.

If you notice effects like these which feel unpleasant, or you think that your heart is often beating too fast, it might be time to cut down on the number of fizzy drinks you're having. You don't have to stop drinking them altogether, but it's definitely a good idea to drink more water during the day than other kinds of drink, including coffee, tea or hot chocolate, which also contain caffeine. And you should avoid having any of these drinks at least six hours before you want to go to sleep. However, if you already drink a lot of caffeine, don't stop suddenly. Doing so can cause headaches, stop you being able to concentrate and make you feel more anxious than usual.

Some studies suggest that you should include some caffeine in your diet because it helps to reduce the possibility of heart problems and developing some kinds of cancer. It can also help you keep going while you exercise and reduce muscle pain after you've worked out. And, of course, it is helpful when you want to stay awake and study when you start yawning!

But how much caffeine is healthy? Doctors say that teenagers shouldn't have more than 100 mg a day, which is about one cup of coffee, or about three cans of regular cola. That isn't to say that drinking three cans of cola is good for you. It contains a lot of sugar and can cause the negative effects mentioned earlier. You should also be very careful with energy drinks. Some large cans can contain over 150 mg of caffeine, which is more than the recommended daily amount for a teenager.

Remember: if your heart often beats fast when you're resting and you don't have fizzy drinks or other drinks containing caffeine, you could have a medical problem. So, if you're even a little bit worried, you should go and ask the doctor to check you over.

2 Read the article again and write true (T) or false (F).

1 Soft drinks such as cola and certain kinds of hot drink have something in common. ....

2 Fizzy drinks have both positive and negative effects on the body. ....

3 The article says you should drink water immediately to reduce the effects of too much caffeine. ....

4 When people try to stop drinking caffeine, they might feel ill. ....

5 Research shows that some caffeine can be healthy for the body. ....

6 Young people shouldn't drink more than one cup of coffee each day. ....

7 Energy drinks contain less caffeine than cola. ....

8 The article says it's a good idea to see a doctor about drinking too much caffeine. ....

3 Match the highlighted words in the article to the meanings.

1 not very nice ....

2 reduce ....

3 have a look at to make sure someone is OK ....

4 disease, illness or injury ....

5 do exercise ....

1 Choose the correct modal verb.

1 Doctors say that we *ought to / shouldn't* eat five pieces of fruit a day.

2 You *don't have to / mustn't* cough without covering your mouth.

3 If you don't feel well, you *don't have to / must* go to school.

4 If you are really sick, you *don't have to / shouldn't* do physical exercise.

5 Most of us *should / don't have to* drink more water.

6 You *must / ought to* call an ambulance, if you think someone is having a heart attack.

7 Your leg is bleeding badly. We *ought to / shouldn't* see a doctor.

8 You *don't have to / mustn't* bring your own lunch if you don't want to.

2 Write the words in the correct order to make sentences.

1 do / has / dinner / to / Jackie / the washing up / after

2 leave / his homework / until / dinner / mustn't / after / Louis

3 the nurse / ought / his arm / Frank / to / to / show

4 The boys / go / to / mustn't / school / sick / they / because / are

5 go / You / in the rain / shouldn't / an umbrella / out / without

6 doesn't / lay / have / the table / Lucinda / to

7 have / the dishwasher / William / put / to / the dishes / in / doesn't

8 ought / to / stop / on / her computer / playing / Rachel

3 Complete the text with the modal verbs in the box.

> don't have to   have to   must
> mustn't   ought to   shouldn't

This month we're making smoothies! A smoothie is fruit with yoghurt or milk. Yum! First, you ¹ _____ get a blender, which mixes food. This is quicker and easier than using sharp knives, which you ² _____ be very careful with. You might find one in the kitchen! Put some yoghurt in the blender and then add the fruit. You ³ _____ spend a lot of money – but you ⁴ _____ try to get fresh fruit because it tastes so good. When you've put the fruit and yoghurt into the blender, you mix it and that's it – easy! It won't take more than two or three minutes! Oh, and you ⁵ _____ let very young children use the blender because it can be dangerous.

4 Complete the conversations with a suitable modal verb and a verb from the box.

> get up (x 2)   go   hit   stop

A: What's wrong with you? You can't stop yawning!

B: I know. I don't understand why I'm so tired. Maybe I ¹ _____ to bed sooner.

A: You go to bed at nine o'clock!

B: Yes, because I ² _____ so early.

A: You ³ _____ early – you do it because you *want* to.

B: Well, I like to do things in the morning before school. But I get plenty of sleep.

A: Maybe the problem's waking up. You ⁴ _____ 'snooze' five times!

B: I know. I ⁵ _____ that because I start to go back to sleep again and then I feel tired.

A: I'm sure that'll make you feel better.

5 Choose the correct sentence in each pair.

1 a I must to go to the dentist's after school, so I'll see you tomorrow.

b I have to go to the dentist's after school, so I'll see you tomorrow.

2 a You don't have to use the computer for a long time because it hurts your eyes.

b You shouldn't use the computer for a long time because it hurts your eyes.

3 a You don't have to go to hospital with a bad cough.

b You don't must go to hospital with a bad cough.

1 Complete the sentences with *thing, where* or *one*.

1 There's some _____ at the door – who do you think it is?

2 I've looked every _____ and I can't find the book.

3 I want to get some _____ special for your birthday.

4 She went to the party, but she didn't know any _____ there.

5 If every _____ helps, it'll be much quicker and easier.

6 I can't find my keys any _____. Have you seen them?

7 No _____ spoke to me all day. It was very quiet.

8 I'm sure your bag is some _____ in the house. Have you looked in your room?

2 Complete the sentences with the words in the box.

anyone	anything	everything
nothing	no one	something

1 This is _____ you need when you send a letter.

2 There's _____ to do while you wait, so take a book with you.

3 Have you got _____ you need to make your pizzas?

4 I don't want to go to a different school because I won't know _____ there.

5 There isn't _____ to eat – we'll have to wait until Mum gets home with the shopping.

6 There's _____ for young people to do in the evening, where I live.

7 The teacher was really angry because _____ did their homework!

LISTENING

PREPARE FOR THE EXAM

Listening Part 1

1 Look at the pictures in 1–7. What can you see? Tell your partner.

1 Where did the girl go to sleep?

2 Why does the girl need to see a doctor?

3 Where do the friends decide to eat today?

4 What should the woman do now?

5 Where will they go for a run this afternoon?

6 Why does the girl think her heart is beating fast?

7 What has the boy done today?

2 For each question, choose the correct answer. Then listen again and check your answers.

03

EXAM TIPS

- Look at the pictures and read the questions carefully.
- Listen for the items in the pictures and choose the picture which answers the question.

VOCABULARY — Music

1 Match the words to their meanings.

1 concert hall	____	a a person who plays recorded songs on the radio or at events
2 DJ	____	b a short recording that you can see on a website
3 celebrity	____	c a person who plays an instrument or sings, especially as part of their job
4 musician	____	d when someone controls how the music is made in a studio
5 guitarist	____	e a TV station that shows mainly music
6 studio	____	f a room where recordings are made
7 festival	____	g a person who plays the guitar
8 live	____	h seen or heard as it happens
9 music channel	____	i a building where you can listen to music
10 sound technician	____	j a person who is famous, especially in entertainment
11 production	____	k a series of special events over several days, usually entertainment
12 clip	____	l a person who checks the quality of sound, often in a studio or at a music event

2 Choose the correct answer.

1 We sat up all night and watched *music videos / lyrics*.
2 I think that seeing *music channel / live music* is the best thing in the world.
3 Do you want to come to 'Jazz in the Grass'? It's a *studio / festival* starting next week.
4 Have you heard the *guitarist / sound technician* on that song?
5 My grandparents never go to *gigs / productions*.
6 I love listening to Pete Frank's choices in the morning – he's such a good *clip / DJ*.
7 There's a beautiful old *concert hall / production* in the city centre.
8 To be a *celebrity / sound technician*, you have to understand how sound works.

3 Complete the article with the words in the box.

> celebrities   DJ   gigs   guitarist   musician
> production   sound technician   studio

Jobs in the **music industry**

Many young people love music and want to work in the music industry when they leave school. Would you like to be the ¹ _____ that everyone listens to in the morning? You can play your favourite music for a job! Or perhaps you've learned to play the guitar at school and have become an excellent ² _____. Of course, the people in these jobs often become famous – they're ³ _____ like actors or sportspeople. But what about other jobs in the industry? There is the ⁴ _____, who has to check hundreds of details in music recordings. Or you could work in ⁵ _____, spending time in a ⁶ _____ with singers or bands. And, of course, somebody has to organise ⁷ _____ for the artists to play in. There are a huge number of jobs available in the music industry and you don't have to be a ⁸ _____ yourself to get into it!

4 Complete the dialogue with words from Exercise 1.

A: You know the band Gogo? Which ¹ _____ do you admire most?
B: I really like Joe Bing, the new ² _____. He plays the guitar so well!
A: I agree! Did you see his latest ³ _____ on the internet last night? Amazing!
B: Yes. It's also been on the ⁴ _____ on TV.
A: Yeah! And did you see that the band is going to be at the music ⁵ _____ in town in the summer? Really exciting!
B: I know! And they're playing inside at the ⁶ _____ in town just before that – and Josh and I have tickets!
A: Oh, you don't! I'm so jealous!

1 Read the article and tick (✓) the ideas that are mentioned.

1 the kinds of music that are recorded at the studio

2 the musicians who have recorded at the studio

3 a way that music is recorded at the studio

4 how the studio became famous

The history of ABBEY ROAD STUDIOS

Abbey Road Studios, where the Beatles recorded most of their work, started its life as a large house, which the record label EMI bought in 1929. The building soon became home to the first purpose-built recording studios in the world, which opened in 1931. Many different types of music have been recorded there, and with its groundbreaking technology, it attracted many big names in the music industry.

In June 1962, the Beatles made their first recording at the studios and between then and 1970, when the band broke up, they recorded 90% of their music in Studio One. The studio is still one of the largest in the world, able to fit a 110-piece orchestra and a 100-person choir at the same time!

The studios developed new ways of producing music, and multi-track recordings (where separate sounds could be recorded and then put together to make a single piece) started to take off because of their innovations. In 1967, the studios and the Beatles made history when the band performed 'All you need is love' live for the first ever satellite TV link-up, which was heard by 350 million people.

The studios really made their name when the Beatles decided to call their second-to-last album *Abbey Road*. Many people consider this to be one of the best albums ever made, and one of the Beatles' most successful. Its cover is recognised all over the world, showing the four musicians crossing the street in front of the studios, guitarist and singer Paul with no shoes on.

As well as the Beatles, many other famous musicians have used the studios to record their songs. These include Oasis, Pink Floyd, the Spice Girls and, more recently, the Killers, Lady Gaga and Coldplay. The studios don't just record music for albums, however. They have also been involved in recording soundtracks for films, perhaps the most famous of which is *Star Wars: Episode 1*.

Because of the studios' close link to the Beatles, many fans of the band go to visit the building. Although it is not possible to go inside the studios, many fans take photos of themselves crossing the road and write graffiti on its garden walls and road signs, remembering the band. Although the studios have struggled in the digital era, they remain a working business, and continue to attract musicians who are keen to follow in the footsteps of the Beatles.

2 Read the article again and correct the information in the following sentences.

1 EMI bought Abbey Road Studios in 1929.

2 Many musicians became famous after recording at Abbey Road Studios.

3 The Beatles recorded their first album in the late 60s.

4 The Beatles helped to produce the first multi-track recordings.

5 The studios asked the Beatles to name an album after them.

6 The studios record films as well as music.

7 Many fans have visited the studios to take tours.

8 The studios have done very well during the digital era.

3 Match the highlighted words and phrases in the article to the meanings.

1 suddenly become successful

2 tried hard to do something difficult

3 do the same thing or job as someone else you know

4 new and a big change from other things of its kind

GRAMMAR — Present perfect and past simple

1 Choose the correct answer.

1 I first *heard / have heard* this song years ago.

2 My favourite band *has played / played* here twice before.

3 There *were / have been* huge crowds last time they were here.

4 Mandy *hasn't listened / didn't listen* to that song last night.

5 Ana can't go to the gig and so she *offered / has offered* her ticket to her friend.

6 *Have you ever played / did you ever play* the violin before?

7 Our music teacher *has recorded / recorded* a song with his band last week.

8 Denis and his friend *performed / have performed* live at their end-of-year concert last week.

2 Read the sentences and put *already*, *just* or *yet* in the right place.

0 Don't put your shoes on the table. I've ^already told you that hundreds of times!

1 Jasmine has bought a new laptop. It's still in the box.

2 I haven't done my homework.

3 I don't want to see that film – I've seen it. Jules and I went last week.

4 Most of our class haven't made their choices for next year.

5 Miguel's phoned. He missed the bus, so he'll be here later.

6 Mum and Dad have seen me perform many times.

7 We haven't chosen our school play.

8 I've heard the most amazing song! Let's find it online.

3 Complete the text with the verb in the simple past or present perfect. Put the adverb in the correct position, where necessary.

I ¹_____ (take part in/just) an amazing arts project, which actually ²_____ (begin) by accident. Perhaps you ³_____ (hear) of the Virtual Choir? A choir is a group of people, who sing together. It all ⁴_____ (start) when musician Eric Whitacre, who ⁵_____ (write) a lot of music, including songs, watched a video clip of a girl singing his music. It ⁶_____ (give) Eric the idea for the virtual choir. I found out about it when I got this message from a friend: 'I ⁷_____ (see/just) this amazing thing. This guy ⁸_____ (invite) people to record their voice and upload it to a site. I ⁹_____ (do/already) mine. Do yours now, then we can be in the same choir.' Nothing unusual about that except that my friend and I live on different sides of the world! And that is how the virtual choir ¹⁰_____ (happen). It's a great experience for people who live far apart!

4 Correct the mistakes in these sentences or put a tick (✓) by any you think are correct.

1 I have just buy a computer game.

2 I have just received your letter.

3 We met at school and since then we are friends.

4 Well, I've met my friends at school seven years ago.

5 I know Claudia since I was a child.

VOCABULARY — Word families

1 Write the correct form of the word in brackets to complete the sentence.

1 The school band made a _____ of a famous song for the school website. (record)

2 The last time I saw a live _____ was in the summer holidays. (perform)

3 I saw a really funny _____ on TV last night. (advertise)

4 Jason is a very _____ person – he can play three instruments. (music)

5 Our teacher _____ the winners of the competition. (announcement)

6 My greatest _____ this year is passing my ballet exam. (achieve)

7 I'd love to work on a cruise ship as an _____. (entertain)

1 Read this advertisement for a music festival and Maria's email. What did she enjoy most at the festival?

Music festival in the Black Mountains

3 days of amazing music from all over the world

Featuring:
Vania from Argentina
The Boys from Estonia
and many more!

Email us for more information

Hi Jake,

I have just returned from an awesome school trip. We got back a couple of days ago and I would like to tell you about it!

We attended the Black Mountains Music Festival, which is held in the Black Mountains in late August. We went with our music class and our music teacher, Ms Jones. She is so cool. The festival takes place every year and it lasts for three days. Musicians come from all over the world, so we heard a lot of different kinds of music. I particularly enjoyed a group from New Zealand – their guitarist was just amazing! Now, I am going to learn how to play the guitar!

Have you ever been to a music festival? Tell me all about it!

Love,

Maria

2 Read the email again. Answer the questions.

1 What phrases does Maria use to start and end the email?

2 Find three adjectives which describe things in an informal way.

3 Write the underlined phrases as short forms.

3 Look at the ways of starting and ending emails. Which words and phrases are suitable for an informal email? Tick (✓) all that apply.

Dear Mr Simpson, … ☐
Hi, Ben! ☐
Hello, Tina, … ☐
Bye for now! ☐
Write soon! ☐
Best regards, … ☐
With best wishes, … ☐

4 Read this email from your English-speaking friend Kim, and the notes you have made. Plan your ideas.

From: Kim

Hi!

Do you remember we talked about going to the music festival in my town? Do you still want to go? —— Yes!

We could go to the festival on Friday or Saturday. Which day would you prefer? —— Say which

What kind of music do you like? I'll find out who's playing and let you know. —— Explain

Would you like to do something in the evening after the festival? —— No, because…

See you soon!

Kim

✅ PREPARE FOR THE EXAM

Writing Part 1

5 Write your email to Kim, using all the notes.

Write about 100 words.
You must use all the notes in the email.
Remember to check your spelling and grammar.

✅ EXAM TIPS

- When you write an email, remember to use suitable phrases to start and end your letter.
- Use short forms and informal words and phrases when you are writing to a friend.

8 AMAZING ARCHITECTURE

VOCABULARY Describing buildings

1 Find adjectives in the word square (→ ↘ ↗ ↓) below to match the meanings.

1 new or different to what was there before ....

2 special and interesting ....

3 comfortable and warm ....

4 done in a certain style for a long time ....

5 relating to the present time, not the past ....

6 important or likely to be important in history ....

7 completely new ....

8 popular for a long time, and of good quality ....

9 extremely good, exciting or surprising ....

10 the earliest form of something ....

s	p	e	c	t	a	c	u	l	a	r	n
o	r	p	k	p	q	z	n	l	n	f	l
r	g	e	c	l	a	s	s	i	c	a	m
i	f	g	c	b	g	v	q	l	n	m	w
g	m	o	d	e	r	n	x	o	c	e	u
i	r	f	r	d	n	d	i	i	n	n	n
n	p	j	l	q	c	t	r	d	b	k	u
a	m	c	z	t	i	o	n	p	f	r	s
l	f	r	k	d	t	a	s	j	r	w	u
j	c	r	a	s	r	h	m	y	e	j	a
m	m	r	i	b	v	f	b	w	s	r	l
j	t	h	m	m	y	m	l	l	h	l	t

2 Choose the correct adjective.

1 My bedroom is very small but *historic / cosy*.

2 Tom and Maggie's home is *unusual / fresh* because it is a boat.

3 This room has *spectacular / historic* views over the mountains.

4 The new museum in town has three lifts on the outside. It's very *modern / brand new*.

5 What an amazing kitchen you've got! It's got a really *brand new / contemporary* style.

6 Be careful with my phone – I got it yesterday, so it's *fresh / brand new*!

7 The mountain village is full of *traditional / fresh* stone cottages.

8 The architect had a lot of *stylish / fresh* ideas for school library books that the students will like.

9 When I visit a town I don't know, I always walk around and look at the *fresh / historic* buildings.

10 I don't think shorts are a very *stylish / historic* thing to wear on a night out.

3 Complete the conversation with the words in the box.

cosy	modern	original	spectacular
traditional	unusual		

Mum: How shall we decorate your new bedroom? The people who lived here before liked strong colours!

Rachel: Yes – I don't want to keep the ¹........................ colour! Can I have blue instead? Maybe a pale blue?

Mum: Yes, that sounds nice. And we could make a feature of the ²........................ view of the mountains from the window, you know, like we saw in that TV programme last night.

Rachel: Oh, yeah! Where they painted the wall with the window in it a different colour. That would be ³......................... I don't know anyone who's got a room like that.

Mum: OK. And what about furniture? Do you want a ⁴........................ style? It's an old house, so that would look nice.

Rachel: Actually, I think I'd prefer something more ⁵........................, you know, up-to-date.

Mum: Sure, well, we can go and have a look at what will fit in the room. It's only a small room, but it's really ⁶........................ and it'll be nice and warm, too.

Rachel: Great! Let's go shopping!

1 Read questions 1–5 quickly. What do all the people want to do?

2 Read about five people who want to decorate their bedrooms (1–5). Decide which shop (A–H) would be the most suitable for each person.

1 Jai wants to create a cosy space. She likes traditional furniture and is looking for some interesting old items which she can put on her walls, as well as a carpet in a light colour. ....

2 Simon wants his bedroom to have a really up-to-date look and wants to paint the walls in bright colours. He likes very modern, unusual furniture. He'd also like something cool to put over his bed. ....

3 Vanessa's room has an old fireplace, which she'd like to make a feature of so her room is really original. She'd love some interesting pictures and she'd also like a lamp which suits the room. ....

4 Samuel has a huge new room to fill. He likes classic furniture and wants somewhere to put his books. He's getting rid of the old carpet, but needs an alternative that looks good and feels comfortable. ....

5 Akiko likes inviting people round to her house. She wants some new curtains in soft colours and would like to cover the walls in similar shades. She's looking for a warm blanket for her sofa, too. ....

- Read about each person and underline what they are looking for.
- Read the options and choose the one which fits each person.

🏠 Home Decoration Shops

A Home
Create a cosy place to hang out with your friends. We have a fantastic new collection of paints in pale colours, as well as a wide range of material in the same colours. Make your own curtains or covers! Our winter range includes wool and other cosy kinds of cloth. Together, we can create a space which reflects your personality.

B Do it Yourself!
We specialise in antiques and have a large selection of furniture for those who wish to create an old-fashioned feel. We are also introducing a range of carpets for the first time in soft shades like cream or pale grey. At the moment, we have some unique decorative wall pieces, too. Come and have a look!

C Decoration Centre
Do you want to create a unique look while keeping the interesting details of an older home? Our design centre will help you make the most of whatever you've got and we'll also look out for paintings which are a little bit different. We have a brand-new section filled with all kinds of lights. They're pretty cool!

D House and Home Store
Here at House and Home Store, we offer a wide collection of super-modern furniture, as well as curtains, carpets and contemporary prints to hang on your walls. If you like to keep things simple and clean, why not take a look at our paint collection, with whites and greys to suit the 'minimalist' look? Your friends will love it!

E Spaces
If you've got a small space you want to make stylish, then come and visit us here at Spaces. You'll be amazed by our modern space-saving furniture, from bookcases and beds to drawers and shelves. We also have a great range of paints and wallpapers in soft colours to make the most of your room. Located next to the antiques centre.

F Inside and Out
We've got a fantastic range of furniture, from extra-large beds and sofas, to shelves and other storage. Perfect for the bigger room. Most of our furniture is made in a traditional design, in wood. We can also offer advice on what to do with your floor and have some great options which don't include carpet.

G Make Your Own Home
If tradition is what you like, take a look at our wide collection of wooden wardrobes, beds and chests of drawers. Coming soon: home decoration section, which will offer a wide variety of paints, wallpaper, lights and pictures.

H ABC Decor
If you love modern things, ABC Decor can help you create the room you've always wanted. We have the latest collections from brilliant contemporary designers and a brand-new selection of paints in bold shades: everything from orange to purple! We also have a second-hand section where we're getting rid of old records – perfect if you have a space to fill on the wall.

1 Complete the table with comparative and superlative adjectives.

	Comparative	Superlative
fresh		
big		
wide		
cosy		
original		
historic		

2 Complete these sentences with the adjective in brackets and (*not*) *as … as, less* or *the least.*

1 In 2019, there was no building in the world, which was .... the Burj Khalifa in Dubai. (tall)

2 I sat in .... chair in the living room because I wanted my visitors to have the best places to sit. (comfortable)

3 This programme is .... last week's. (not good)

4 That film was .... one I've ever seen. So boring! (exciting)

5 Filipa is .... than Joana; Filipa is very quiet. (lively)

6 Some people write about really crazy things online. I found a blog about .... musical instruments to play round a campfire! (acceptable)

3 Write sentences about the information in the table, using the words below to help you.

	city	*holiday resort*	*theme park*
weather	☀	☀ ☀	☀ ☀ ☀
price	€€€	€€€€	€€
historic	✓✓✓✓	✓	✓
exciting	✓	✓✓	✓✓✓✓

0 weather / good / holiday resort / city
The weather is better at the holiday resort than in the city.

1 city / holiday resort / expensive
....

2 theme park / expensive
....

3 theme park / historic / holiday resort
....

4 city / historic
....

5 city / exciting
....

6 theme park / exciting / holiday resort
....

4 Correct the mistakes in these sentences or put a tick (✓) by any you think are correct.

◉ **1** Smaller cities are more nice than very big ones.
....

2 She is one of the most important people in my life.
....

3 Our new flat is farer from the city centre than the old one.
....

4 The better thing I've ever done is design my own bedroom.
....

5 She is the funniest person I have ever known!
....

1 Are the adjectives in bold strong or normal? Write *S* for strong or *N* for normal.

1 I'm **exhausted**! I've just finished painting the hall.
2 There's an **old** castle in our town. It's a few hundred years old.
3 Our flat is really hot in summer, but **freezing** in winter.
4 Wow! What a **good** view.
5 I feel **terrible**. I think I'm getting a cold.
6 My dad designs buildings – they're **spectacular**!

2 Circle the correct adverb.

1 I'm *incredibly* / *absolutely* tired. I think I'll go to bed early.
2 Sara's feeling *absolutely* / *very* happy because she's passed her exams.
3 Our hotel room was *extremely* / *absolutely* big with views of the sea.
4 Jenny's parents' house is *absolutely* / *very* enormous.
5 That meal was *absolutely* / *incredibly* tasty – thanks!
6 I've painted my room, but it looks *really* / *absolutely* bad.

LISTENING

 1 Listen to six conversations. What are they about? Choose the correct answer for each one.

1 a description of the boy's house / how to get to the boy's house
2 how to decorate a bedroom / what a bedroom looks like
3 what some homework is about / an idea for some classwork
4 what they are going to do / where they have been
5 what they have found today / what they are going to look for
6 why a house is good / why someone built a house

PREPARE FOR THE EXAM

Listening Part 2

2 Now read the questions. Listen to the six conversations again. For each question, choose the correct answer.

1 You will hear a boy telling his friend about his new house.
What does he say about it?
A It isn't as interesting as where he used to live.
B His bedroom is not as good as his old one.
C There is less space in the garden than at the old house.

2 You will hear a brother and sister talking about the girl's bedroom.
What does the girl like about it?
A its original decoration
B its contemporary furniture
C its spectacular views

3 You hear two students talking about a design project they have to do.
How do they both feel about it?
A It's less interesting than they expected.
B It's difficult to think of ideas for it.
C It's challenging to do in the time available.

4 You will hear two friends talking about a trip they have been on.
What does the boy say about it?
A He liked the accommodation.
B He enjoyed getting to know a new city.
C He found the whole experience very tiring.

5 You will hear two friends talking about a project they will work on.
How do they both feel about it?
A keen to see the remains of an ancient village
B hopeful of finding interesting pots from the past
C excited about looking for coins they haven't seen before

6 You will hear a boy telling a friend about a house.
What does he like best about it?
A its design
B its location
C its size

EXAM TIPS

- You have to choose the correct option from a set of three. When you listen the first time, try to think about what the speaker or speakers are talking about.
- In the second listening, choose the option that correctly answers the question.

9 THE FUTURE IS NOW

VOCABULARY Technology

1 Write the letters in the correct order to make words. Complete the sentences.

1 lsdpiay
I can't see the _____ on my phone because the screen's broken.

2 eeterpminx
We're going to do an _____ in chemistry tomorrow.

3 cioncetonn
When there's a storm the internet _____ is very poor.

4 etvionnin
The best _____ is the smartphone.

5 glup ni
You need to _____ electrical items or they won't work!

6 slittelea
The information for the weather forecast comes from a _____ in the sky.

7 lefu
Drivers are complaining about the price of _____.

8 ehgrca
Don't forget to _____ your phone or the battery will run out.

9 mupp
In some countries, there might be a village _____ to get water from the ground.

10 eworp
Turn off the _____ at the main switch.

2 Choose the correct answer.

1 It's a good idea to carry a *pump* / *plug* on your bike at all times.

2 The *power* / *fuel* that Dad puts in his car is good for the environment.

3 Sam hasn't got a very good internet *connection* / *invention* at home.

4 Let me *plug in* / *power* my laptop and we can do some online shopping!

5 A light's come on in the *connection* / *display* in the car. Is there something wrong?

6 Uh oh! The lights have gone out again. It must be another problem with the *experiment* / *power*.

7 The first *satellite* / *experiment* went into space in 1957.

8 I've just read about an *experiment* / *invention*, which says you can cook an egg between two mobile phones – it isn't true!

9 The best *invention* / *connection* would be something that automatically does your homework for you!

10 My tablet's just turned itself off. I think it needs *charging* / *connection*.

3 Read the short texts and match them to the words from Exercises 1 and 2.

This is what we call electricity. Sometimes it goes off, or stops working, and people aren't able to use devices which need to be plugged in.
1 _____

Many modern electronic devices have one of these. It includes icons, words and so on, which show you what the device can do and how to use it.
2 _____

This is a piece of equipment that is sent into space to collect information about the weather and is also used for communication.
3 _____

Scientists and governments are always looking for new forms of this. This is because we are using too much of it, and we have to look for types that can be used again and again.
4 _____

I've got one of these with my bike. I use it when the tyres don't have much air in them.
5 _____

READING

1 You are going to read an article about computer games. Look at the picture and the title. What do you think the article will explain? Read the article quickly to check your ideas.

RACING GAMES

Last year's new racing games were so good, I wasn't sure that this year's could be any better – but actually, they are! *Onrush* is a brilliant game, which is really realistic and great to look at. It's also really fun, which makes a change from some of the similar hi-tech games out there. In the game, you have to drive as fast as you can around the track, but you also have to complete objectives, such as doing tricks or trying to get the people you're racing against off the track in order to win points. It's all action!

Next, *The Crew 2*. In this game, you can ride around in some amazing vehicles, including a Porsche and Mazda – but you also get to drive a boat and fly a plane. The crazy bit is that you change between vehicles as you play, without having to press pause. You travel across the whole of the USA – just like the original game, the sights are fantastic, and you can also attend events, including motocross and Formula 1-style races. The first version of the game had some technical issues, so it's great to see that these have all been resolved.

If you're into motorbikes, then *TT Isle of Man: Ride on the Edge* is for you! The real TT races take place on a small island, where motorcyclists race around the roads at up to 321 km per hour. They travel along country roads and through towns and villages at incredible speeds on first-class bikes. Now you can try it out for yourself and experience how absolutely amazing it is to race at top speed! You can even choose which top TT rider to be in the game, and belong to one of the most famous teams.

My final choice is *Gravel*. This game's about off-road racing, and this time you try to become the best at driving through forests, mountains, deserts and many other landscapes. There are lots of events to go to, but you'll have to be the top racer to win them all because there are more than two hundred! These take place in stadiums and on tracks – it really is extreme and something everybody wants to be the best at! It isn't the cheapest game, but it looks fun!

 PREPARE FOR THE EXAM

Reading Part 3

2 Read the article and the questions below. For each question, choose the correct answer.

1 What does Ella say about the *Onrush* game?
   A It has the best graphics she has ever seen.
   B It is less serious than other games of its type.
   C It can be very hard to beat competitors.
   D It is difficult trying to do the tricks.

2 Why does Ella say *The Crew 2* is better than the original game?
   A It has more competitions to take part in.
   B The vehicles are more interesting.
   C The scenery is more exciting.
   D It works without problems.

3 What does Ella think is exciting about playing the TT game?
   A the speeds you can travel at
   B the bikes you can ride
   C the racers you can pretend to be
   D the track you can race on

4 How does Ella feel about the game *Gravel*?
   A pleased about its low price
   B enthusiastic about the way it looks
   C excited by the challenge it provides
   D disappointed by how many competitions it has

5 Which description could be used at the beginning of this article?
   A *Ella Jones: creator of exciting video games.*
   B *Ella Jones reviews some of this year's best games.*
   C *Ella Jones speaks to video games producers about their new games.*
   D *Ella Jones visits some of the top race tracks that games are based on.*

 EXAM TIPS

- Read the text and think carefully about the meaning.
- Then, read the questions and options and identify the place in the text which answers each question. Remember that the words and phrases used in the text may be different from those in the questions and options.

3 Match the highlighted words and phrases in the article to the meanings.

1 using a vehicle or bike on rough ground
2 cars, buses etc. which take people from one place to another
3 very good, exciting or large
4 something done to entertain people
5 seeming true to life

1 Choose the correct answers.

1 Ask Jamie – *he'll / he's going to* help you with your project.
2 After school, *we're going to / we'll* hang out in the town centre. Come and join us.
3 Which of these devices *are replacing / will replace* phones by the year 2050?
4 I'm sorry, but I'm not free on Monday as *I'm meeting / I'll meet* Sophia.
5 So, *I'm going to tell / I'm telling* you about the most amazing invention.
6 *We're uploading / we upload* all the new information to the website right now.

2 Complete the conversations with the future continuous of the verbs in brackets.

1 **A:** What will you be doing this time next year?
   B: _____ (study) even harder!
2 **A:** Do you think that Mr Jones has marked our work yet?
   B: Someone told me that _____ (do) it over the weekend.
3 **A:** Will you stay in touch while you're at your cousins' house?
   B: Yes, _____ (write) my blog every day.
4 **A:** I can't wait for the holidays to start!
   B: Same here! This time next week _____ (swim) in the sea!
5 **A:** Have you invited anyone to your party yet?
   B: _____ (send) a Facebook invite tonight!

3 Read about Jyra and complete the text with the verbs in the correct future form. More than one answer may be correct.

Tomorrow we [1] _____ (present) our ideas for technology in the future to the whole school. But first, some ideas! There are lots of exciting things that we think [2] _____ (happen) within the next five years. Over the next few years, scientists and inventors [3] _____ (develop) new things for every aspect of our lives – the environment, communication, travel. It's likely that scientists [4] _____ (find) fuels that are completely renewable. Also, it seems that they [5] _____ (invent) cars that don't need any fuel at all!
As for communication, we all know about smartphones but did you know that next week Apple [6] _____ (look at) 1,000 new apps. That's the number of apps that inventors send in every week! How [7] _____ (our children/communicate) with each other? [8] _____ (we/tell) them to stop looking at their phones? Who knows?! It's the future and it's exciting!

4 Complete the sentences about the future. Use a suitable future form and the words in brackets to help you.

1 By 2050 we _____.
   (drive / electric cars)
2 In the future people _____.
   (wear / computers / on arms)
3 We probably _____.
   (not / live / on the Moon)
4 Most people believe that we
   _____.
   (live / longer lives)

5 Correct the mistakes in these sentences or put a tick (✓) by any you think are correct.

1 I bring the food and you can bring something to drink.
   _____
2 Our relationship going to last forever!
   _____
3 Give me a ring if you are coming.
   _____
4 Tomorrow we go to the pool and I know that will be a fantastic day.
   _____
5 At the weekend, we are going to had a party.
   _____

1 Write the words in the correct order to make sentences.

1 latest / isn't / The / very / phone / going to be / small
2 expensive / apps / too / Some / just / are
3 doesn't / on / mobile phone / long / The / last / power / enough / my
4 hasn't / got / Harry / to / go / money / enough / to the cinema
5 was / first prize / win / to / slow / Svetlana / too
6 tests / Next / are / important / term's / very

2 Complete the sentences with *too*, *enough* or *very*.

1 Dylan is a _____ good friend.
2 He's often _____ busy to see me because he paints a lot.
3 His pictures are _____ artistic.
4 Unfortunately, his portraits aren't good _____ for the competition.
5 They are _____ strange for a lot ovpeople.

1 Look at the pictures. Do you own any of these devices? Which do you use most often?

2 There is one mistake in each of these sentences. The mistake can be grammar, spelling, punctuation, word order or vocabulary. Correct the mistakes.

1 Smartphones continue to get faster and better in the future.

2 Although the TV is a good product, the screen is not enough big.

3 People spend very much time on their gadgets and don't do anything else.

4 So, what should you do if you lose your mobil fone or any other device?

5 Do you think people learn anything interesting when they play computer games!

6 Laptops have pretty good hearing these days. Their speakers are better than they were.

7 Tablets comes in all shapes and sizes.

8 How do you chose which headphones to buy?

3 Read the task and a student's answer. Find and correct seven mistakes.

My favourite device

What's your favourite electronic device? Why?

Do you think people spend too much time on their devices?

The device I like best is probably my tablet. I'm on it most of the time when I'm not at school or playing football. I like them because it's smaller than my laptop, so can I carry it around with me. It's larger than my phone which means I can look things better on the screan.

I think the idea that people spends too much time on their devices is a bit oldfashioned. They're just part of our lives and they do so many amazing things. We can message people instantly, upload photos to social media, and many other things we wouldn't be able do without them.

PREPARE FOR THE EXAM

Writing Part 2 (An article)

4 Read this exam task. Write one or two sentences to answer each question.

You see this notice on an English-language website.

ARTICLES WANTED!

Fantastic apps

What app do you use that you would recommend to your friends? Why?

What apps do you think there will be in the future?

Tell us what you think!

Write an article answering these questions and we will post the best ones on our website next month.

5 Now write your article.

- Remember to answer all the questions – use your ideas from exercise 4.
- Remember to check your spelling and grammar.
- Write about 100 words.

EXAM TIPS

- You may have to answer questions in this part of the test. You must answer all of these questions.
- Make notes of one or two ways of answering each question before you write your final answer.

10 ANIMALS IN DANGER

1 Look at these photos. Choose a word from the box to label each one.

| creatures | crops | humans | jungle | landscape | rainforest |

A

B

C

....

....

....

D

E

F

....

....

....

2 Now match the words from Exercise 1 and other words you know to these meanings.

1 a plant, such as grain, fruit or vegetables, grown in large quantities

....

2 the number of people living in a particular area

....

3 animals or plants that may soon not exist because there aren't many of them left

....

4 a forest in a tropical area which receives a lot of rain

....

5 the natural environment of an animal or plant

....

6 the activity of killing animals, either by humans or other animals, usually for food

....

7 the appearance of an area of land, especially in the countryside

....

8 air, land and water where people, animals and plants live

....

3 Complete the text with words from Exercises 1 and 2.

When we think of Australia, we often think of beaches or the Sydney Harbour Bridge. But in the north of Queensland, there is a completely different [0] _environment_ to discover: the Daintree Forest. This is the largest area of tropical [1] .... on the Australian continent and besides this, it is the oldest in the world. Very few [2] .... live here; in fact the whole [3] .... of the area is only about 500 people.

However, there are lots of interesting [4] .... here, and the forest is the [5] .... of the southern Cassowary bird. Not only is it the third largest bird species in the world, it is unfortunately [6] ...., too. This is not because of [7] ...., but the fact that the areas they live in have been reduced in size. The forest and the animals which live in it are now protected to stop further problems.

The [8] .... includes mountains that go all the way down to the sea, where you can find some of the most beautiful beaches in the world. This area is really unusual in its plants and wildlife and now there are also large [9] .... of cocoa trees, which chocolate is made from. You'll taste the best chocolate here! So, why not visit this amazing place and experience something new and exciting?

1 Read the first paragraph of an article about an event Grace Rees took part in. What do people do for this event?

2 Read the rest of the article about Grace Rees and answer the question.

Grace Rees is going green!

Grace Rees has recently taken part in Clean Up Australia Day. She spent the day collecting drinks containers, sweet wrappers and small pieces of paper from a beach near her home.

Grace has been involved in this event for about five years now. 'I've always done it with my school, but this year my friends and I decided to register as our own group. We think it's good not only to pick up the rubbish, but to bring people's attention to the fact that there is a lot of rubbish out there. If you do it with friends and family, then it means you can have fun and do something useful at the same time. It's an important thing to do. We have such a beautiful environment, and rubbish spoils it.'

1 What is Grace's attitude towards Clean Up Australia Day?
A She doesn't particularly enjoy the tasks she has to do.
B She thinks schools should allow students time off to take part in it.
C She sees it as an opportunity to tell other people about rubbish problems.

Clean Up Australia Day

The first Clean Up Day event took place in Sydney in 1989, when Australian Ian Kiernan, who had just sailed around the world, decided to take action for something he felt strongly about: the amount of plastic pollution in ocean ¹ _____. He was worried that the polluted seas were affecting sea ² _____ and that this was leading to some of them becoming ³ _____.

The following year, the day became known as Clean Up Australia Day, and people all over the continent joined in to collect rubbish. Every year, more and more of the ⁴ _____ take part, and today it is one of the most successful community events which improve the ⁵ _____.

In 2000, the event became Clean Up The World and over 40 million volunteers from over 120 countries took part to change the look of the ⁶ _____, getting rid of huge amounts of rubbish.

PREPARE FOR THE EXAM

Reading Part 5

3 Read the article about how Clean Up Australia Day started, and choose the correct word for each gap.

1 A places   B habitats
   C locations   D societies
2 A creatures   B bodies
   C pets   D things
3 A gone   B disappeared
   C endangered   D warned
4 A human   B person
   C man   D population
5 A environment   B climate
   C situation   D location
6 A view   B scenery
   C landscape   D picture

EXAM TIPS

- In this part of the test, you have to complete a text with missing words. You have four options to choose from for each word that is missing.
- Read the whole text for meaning before choosing your answers. Then read through it again at the end, to make sure the answers you've chosen fit well.

4 Read both articles about Clean Up Australia Day and answer the questions.

1 Ian Kiernan began the event because
   A he realised that some sea creatures had disappeared.
   B he thought people were using too much plastic.
   C he noticed that other countries were much cleaner.
2 Which comment best describes the Clean Up Australia Day event?
   A It's a great day for the families to meet up to discuss their problems.
   B It's a time when people listen to Ian Kiernan's talk about the environment.
   C It's a period of time when people work together to achieve something good.

5 Match the highlighted words in the second article to the meanings.

1 have clear opinions   _____
2 group of people with similar interests   _____
3 having an influence on   _____
4 go in a direction   _____
5 do something to solve a problem   _____

1 Write the words in the correct order to make sentences. Add a comma (,) in the correct place.

0 won / If / the lottery / I / a boat / I / would / buy
If I won the lottery, I would buy a boat.

1 I / If / a boat / another country / bought / would / I / sail / to
....

2 I / sailed / visit / would / I / If / a lot of / countries / different
....

3 visited / I / If / a lot of / would / different places / I / photos / take
....

4 I / If / took / put / photos / I / on my blog / would / them
....

5 If / put / I / them / on my blog / my amazing trip / everyone / see / would
....

6 pleased / If / very / they / them / be / I / liked / would
....

2 Match the beginnings and endings of the sentences.

1 If I go to Africa, ...
2 If I won a million dollars, ...
3 Unless you phone the bus company, ...
4 If people recycle more things, ...
5 If you threw the paper cups in the recycling, ...
6 When Mark finds injured animals on the roads, ...
7 If we had our own vegetable garden, ...
8 If everyone turned off the lights, ...

a our electricity bill would be lower.
b he takes them to the vet.
c you won't get your umbrella back.
d we wouldn't need to buy as much food at the supermarket.
e I'll go on a safari.
f there'll be less rubbish to bury.
g they'd become different paper products.
h I'd go round the world on a cruise.

3 Complete the sentences with the correct form of the verbs in brackets.

1 If you joined the basketball team, you .... (enjoy) it.
2 If you ask Molly, she .... (help) you.
3 If you don't do your homework regularly, you .... (fall) behind everyone else.
4 When we go to the safari park, we .... (see) the big cats.
5 If you heat water, it .... (boil) at 100°C.
6 If I got the top mark in the class, I .... (be) very pleased with myself.
7 If you wanted to help out, you .... (have) to sign up first.
8 If you don't hurry, you .... (miss) the bus.

4 Complete the second sentence so that it means the same as the first.

0 Unless we help animals in danger, they will disappear.
If *we don't help animals in danger* , they will disappear.

1 If he doesn't work hard, he won't pass the exam.
Unless ...., he won't pass the exam.

2 Unless it rains tomorrow, I'll play tennis.
If ...., I'll play tennis.

3 If you don't listen to the teacher, you won't know what to do.
Unless ...., you won't know what to do.

4 Unless we start growing our own food, we'll continue to spend a lot of money at supermarkets.
If ...., we'll continue to spend a lot of money at supermarkets.

5 If we don't do more to protect our environment, we won't be able to save more animals.
Unless ...., we won't be able to save more animals.

5 Correct the mistakes in these sentences or put a tick (✓) by any you think are correct.

1 I remembered that if I don't do my work, they would not let me go on the school trip.
....

2 Next weekend I have nothing to do so when you want, you can come to visit   me.
....

3 If you come to the party with me, it will be better.
....

4 My parents would be very happy if you accept the invitation.
....

5 I think if you met him, you would like him.
....

6 Unless you help on the clean-up day, we won't have enough volunteers.
....

1 Match the phrases to their meanings.

1 at least ....
2 at first ....
3 at its best ....
4 at risk ....
5 at present ....
6 at once ....
7 at long last ....

a finally
b now
c immediately
d when you are telling someone about an advantage in a bad situation
e in danger
f at the beginning of a situation or period
g at the highest level of achievement or quality

2 Complete the email with phrases with *at*.

To: Darcie
From: Sunny

Hi Darcie,

Something strange just happened.

I heard this loud bang and
1 .... I didn't
know what it was. I looked out
of the window and I couldn't see
anything unusual, so I carried on
doing my homework. Then I heard
the bang again and I ran downstairs
2 .... to
get Dad. I wanted to know that
3 .... it wasn't
just me that heard it. Dad said,
'A bird's just flown into the window,
twice! It's still a bit confused
4 .... but it
will be OK.'

We waited for quite a long time, but
5 .... the bird
was fine again and flew off.

How was your day?!

I hope to hear from you soon.

Sunny

1 Look at these photos. They were all in a competition called *The changing planet*. Which do you like best and why?

I like a / b / c best because ....

2 You will hear a conversation between a boy and a girl who attended an exhibition which displayed photos a–c in a competition. What do you think they are going to talk about? Tick the topics.

the number of people there ☐
rainforests ☐
different types of camera ☐
people changing photos ☐
features of a good photograph ☐
how to take a good photograph ☐

🔊 3 Listen and check your answers.

🔊 4 Listen to the conversation again. Decide whether each sentence is true (T) or false (F).

1 Lindsay found the exhibition too crowded. ....
2 Ben enjoyed the photos that were taken in a hot, wet place. ....
3 Lindsay thought that the best picture was a water scene. ....
4 Ben suggests that Lindsay's favourite photo was changed in some way. ....
5 Lindsay thinks the desert picture was an original subject. ....
6 Both Ben and Lindsay are excited to find out who will win the competition. ....

11 OFF TO SCHOOL

VOCABULARY School

1 Write the letters in the correct order to make words.

1 eary _____
2 ripamry _____
3 scanderyo _____
4 qsuonitacifail _____
5 gniroadb hcolos _____

6 uaetgrdadnreu _____
7 edeegr _____
8 tadten _____
9 rekab pu _____
10 uticaoned _____

2 Complete the sentences with the correct form of words from Exercise 1.

1 I went to _____ because my parents went to live abroad, but I wanted to stay in my own country.
2 I worked hard at university and I was really pleased with my result. I got a first-class _____.
3 My birthday was never during school time. We always _____ the week before.
4 The teachers always checked that everyone was in class. You have to _____ school by law.
5 I enjoyed being an _____ at university. I worked hard but had a lot of fun, too.
6 We were in _____ seven at school when we started learning biology.

3 Complete the comment with the correct form of words in the box.

attend   break up   degree   do badly   do well   education
primary   qualifications   secondary   Year

Tell us how you feel about SCHOOL

When I was six, I went to [1] _____ school. I enjoyed it because in the first [2] _____, everyone looked after us. We didn't have homework but we had to [3] _____ in all our subjects, and the teachers helped us. At the age of 11, I changed schools and went to [4] _____ school. That was hard because I didn't have any friends. I didn't like it and I [5] _____ in the first tests. When we [6] _____ for the holidays, I had to have extra lessons. I didn't want to go back to school but I had to [7] _____. Fortunately, now I'm in Year 12 and things are different. These days I love school, have lots of friends, and I'm studying hard. I want to go on to university and get a first-class [8] _____ in design. It's really important to get good [9] _____ these days to find a good job. It just shows you how important [10] _____ is!

Jodie, aged 15

44   UNIT 11

1 How many students are there in your school?

fewer than 500 ☐   500 to 1000 ☐   more than 1000 ☐

Do you think your school is a big school?

2 Read the article below quickly and complete the title.

3 Read the article again. Look at the sentences below and decide if each sentence is correct or incorrect. Write C for correct or I for incorrect.

1 People usually call the City Montessori School by the first letters of its name.
2 The first five students at the school were relatives of Dr Gandhi.
3 The school buildings are situated in several towns.
4 Professor Geeta Kingdon thinks it would be too difficult to organise a meeting of all the students.
5 The school has increased in size quite slowly.
6 Dr Gandhi recognises that many people have helped in the school's success.
7 The school fees are quite high and difficult to afford.
8 If a student is having difficulties at home, there is someone to talk to.
9 The school received a negative report from UNESCO.
10 The school sometimes has teachers and students from other countries.

The _____ school in the world

The first day at school can be quite scary for any pupil but imagine being one among 50,000 or more! That is the total number of students at the City Montessori School in Lucknow, India. The school, better known as CMS, employs 4,500 staff including teachers, support staff, and others such as cleaners and gardeners.

The school was set up by husband and wife team Dr Jagdish Gandhi and Bharti Gandhi in 1959. The first pupils were the children of family members – and there were only five of them. As time went by, more people started to hear about the school and they wanted their children to attend. Slowly, the numbers rose. Today there are about 20 sites around Lucknow and the school's population is bigger than that of some towns. The school educates students between the ages of 3 and 17. They all wear a uniform and each class has about 45 pupils. But due to the size of the school, it is never possible for everyone to meet as there is no place that is big enough for everyone to fit in. One of the school's heads, Dr Gandhi's daughter Geeta Kingdon, said in an interview that, 'The whole of Lucknow would be jammed if we tried because one bus holds 50 children, so we'd need 1,000 buses to bring everyone together.'

In 2013, the speed at which the school grew was recognised by the *Guinness Book of Records*. It was a proud moment for the school, and was because of the efforts of parents, pupils and teachers, said Dr Gandhi. The school doesn't receive any money from the government and the children's parents are only charged a small amount for their children to attend.

For each pupil, there is also one teacher responsible for his or her health and life outside the classroom. In this way, the staff believe that no one is forgotten. Besides the traditional subjects such as maths, English and geography, the students also learn about world peace. CMS is the only school in the world to be awarded a UNESCO Peace Prize for Education for its efforts in this field.

Today, the school is famous for its exam results and its international exchange programmes. The school has some well-respected past students, who have gone on to work in international organisations. However, within the school, and especially with everyone wearing the same uniform, it can be difficult to get noticed, so the students have to work especially hard. Dr Gandhi believes that the children receive not only an education, but also a love of the world.

4 Match the highlighted words in the article to the meanings.

1 the energy that you need to do something
2 have someone work or do a job for you and pay them for it
3 following the customs or ways of behaving that have continued in a group of people or society for a long time
4 happened or existed before now
5 feeling very pleased about something

GRAMMAR   Past perfect

1 Complete the sentences. Use the words in brackets with the verb in the past perfect.

0 When Max arrived home, his parents
had taken his brother to the swimming pool .
(take / brother / to the swimming pool)

1 Alice didn't want to go to the museum
because she _____.
(go there / on / school trip)

2 Kelly wasn't allowed to do sports because
she _____. (forget /
trainers).

3 Frank turned on his Xbox after he
_____. (complete /
all / homework)

4 I gave Jenny a book for her birthday but
she _____. (already
read / it)

5 Kevin didn't have any homework because
he _____. (finish /
it / school)

6 Luisa repeated the test because she
_____. (not / do well /
the first time)

7 Mario was tired because he
_____. (not / sleep /
all night)

8 When I got off the train at the station,
my parents _____.
(not / arrive / to meet me)

2 Choose the correct answer.

Last week I ¹ *had / had had* a terrible
day. First, I ² *woke / had woken* up late
and so by the time I reached the bus
stop to go to school, the bus ³ *already
left / had already left*. Our neighbour
was just leaving her house, so she
⁴ *offered / had offered* to take me to
school. Unfortunately, there was a lot
of traffic and nothing ⁵ *moved / had
moved* for about 30 minutes. I wanted
to send my friend a text, but then I
⁶ *realised / had realised* that I ⁷ *left /
had left* my phone on the kitchen table.
Finally, when I ⁸ *got / had got* to school,
the bell ⁹ *didn't ring / hadn't rung* yet,
which was strange. I went inside the
school and looked at the clock in the
school hall, and then I understood – the
clocks ¹⁰ *went / had gone* back by an
hour and so, in fact, I wasn't late at all!

3 The short forms of *had* and of *would* are both *'d*. Does *'d* in these sentences mean *had* or *would*?

	had	would
1 I'd like to go now.	☐	☐
2 If I went there, I'd call you for sure!	☐	☐
3 They'd just spoken to him.	☐	☐
4 I'd just bought an umbrella.	☐	☐
5 They'd met each other earlier.	☐	☐
6 He'd do it if he had some money.	☐	☐

4 Complete the questions with the simple past or past perfect form of the verb.

1 **A:** Where _____ (you / meet) your new
friend Jack for the first time?
B: On holiday in Spain.

2 **A:** What birthday present _____
(his parents / give) him a few weeks earlier?
B: A trip to Spain to visit his uncle.

3 **A:** _____ (he / ever be) abroad before?
B: Yes, once, to Florida.

4 **A:** _____ (his friends / not / organise)
a party for his birthday?
B: Yes, a surprise party!

5 **A:** When _____ (they / tell) him that
they had organised a party for him?
B: Two weeks before his birthday, when he told them about
the trip to Spain.

6 **A:** How _____ (Jack / feel)?
B: Sad, because he wanted to do both things!

7 **A:** _____ (his parents / already / book)
his flight?
B: Yes, and paid for it.

8 **A:** So what _____ (his friends / do) in
the end?
B: They decided to have the party when Jack got back
home, so he was very happy!

5 Choose the correct sentence in each pair.

◉ **1** **a** I went downstairs and was happy to find out that my
mum made roast beef.
b I went downstairs and was happy to find out that my
mum had made roast beef.

2 **a** After the match had ended, I had the opportunity to
see the soccer players.
b After the match was ended, I had the opportunity to
see the soccer players.

3 **a** After our teacher had told us the rules, we started
to play.
b After the teacher told us the rules, we had started
to play.

4 **a** When she got home, she realised that her parents
bought her a puppy.
b When she got home, she realised that her parents had
bought her a puppy.

5 **a** In the evening, she turned on the TV and realised that
she had won the lottery.
b In the evening, she turned on the TV and realised that
she won the lottery.

VOCABULARY Compound nouns

1 Complete the words by adding the vowels.

1 t __ m __ t __ bl __
2 l __ nch t __ m __
3 b __ s st __ ck __ t
4 h __ __ ad t __ __ ch __ r
5 br __ __ k t __ m __
6 h __ m __ w __ rk
7 bl __ ckb __ __ rd
8 t __ xtb __ __ k

WRITING A story (2)

>> See *Prepare to write* box, Student's Book page 67.

1 How do you feel when you are going to take an exam or test?

happy ☐   sad ☐   scared ☐   frightened ☐   nervous ☐   excited ☐

2 Read Katie's story and answer the questions.

1 What subject was the exam in?

2 How had Katie prepared for the exam?

3 What did students do before the exam?

4 Why did the teacher go red?

Something really funny happened in an exam last week. It was our end-of-year biology exam and we were all very nervous. I had studied really hard, but I really wasn't looking forward to it. The teacher read out the instructions carefully, but she didn't repeat what she had told us the day before: 'If your mobile phone rings, you will fail the exam.' Of course, we all looked at our phones and made sure we'd turned them off anyway!

We started the exam. Suddenly, a phone rang. Everyone looked around to see whose phone it was. Then we all noticed the teacher looking extremely red. We laughed so much! Even teachers forget things!

3 Read these sentences. Look at the adjectives or adverbs underneath them and choose the two that are possible in the gap.

0 The door started to open and everyone looked at it *excitedly / curiously* .
excitedly   curiously   differently

1 She refused to put her bag on the _____ floor.
delicious   dusty   dirty

2 The people left the house _____ after the party.
secretly   quietly   completely

3 My friend gave me a _____ present.
painful   brand new   magnificent

4 We walked into class _____ before our test.
nervously   extremely   quickly

PREPARE FOR THE EXAM

Writing Part 2 (A story)

4 Your English teacher has asked you to write a story. Your story must begin with this sentence:

Joshua looked at the board, where his teacher had posted the exam results.

Write your story. Make it as interesting as you can.

- Use adjectives and adverbs.
- Write about 100 words.
- Remember to check your spelling and grammar.

EXAM TIPS

- Use a variety of tenses and vocabulary to keep readers interested in your story.
- When you have finished, check your story carefully for grammar and spelling.

12 GETTING AROUND

VOCABULARY · Travel

1 Label the pictures with some of the words from the box.

| abroad | check in | land | reach | sail | tour | unpack |

1 ....

2 ....

3 ....

4 ....

5 ....

2 Match the beginnings and endings of the sentences.

1 We're going on holiday tomorrow and ....
2 We're going to France and we're excited ....
3 Are you going ....
4 Sorry we're late – we got ....
5 What time will the train ....

a because we've never been abroad before.
b setting off very early.
c away on holiday this year?
d reach Edinburgh?
e held up on the motorway.

3 Choose the correct answer.

1 We should get to the airport early, so we have plenty of time to ....
  a be held up   **b** go away   **c** check in
2 My friend Josh wants to study .... next year and he's thinking about the USA.
  a on board   **b** abroad   **c** aboard
3 What time does your plane .... ?
  a land   **b** check in   **c** reach
4 What time does the .... of the city start?
  a tourist   **b** touring   **c** tour
5 The girls .... this morning at sunrise to catch the early ferry.
  a landed   **b** set off   **c** went away
6 Jane is .... for a week and I'm looking after her pet cats.
  a going away   **b** setting out   **c** landing
7 When we arrive at the hotel, we'll .... our cases and then go to the pool.
  a reach   **b** unpack   **c** check in
8 My parents want to .... around the Greek islands on holiday this year.
  a set off   **b** land   **c** sail
9 When we .... Paris, we'll get a taxi to our apartment.
  a land   **b** reach   **c** sail
10 We got .... at the airport waiting for our bags to appear.
  a held up   **b** set off   **c** went away

1 Look at the texts below. What kind of texts are they?

LANDSPORTS

Whatever your game, we've got it at the Landsports club! Beach volleyball lovers will enjoy playing on soft white sand, there are tennis courts with spectacular views, and if it's your brain that needs to play, then we've got outdoor chess, too! Check in for two hours of fun.

TASTY

Do you want to learn how to cook delicious dishes using local ingredients? We take you up to a restaurant in the mountains for a fun afternoon that will give you lots of new ideas and help with basic cooking skills. You're sure to please your family with the results when you get back home!

ON THE SOFA

Call in at our popular club and café near the harbour and enjoy free online access for as long as you want. We have a huge variety of board games available that are suitable for all ages and skill levels. You can test your own ability or invite friends and family to play against you.

FLOCKO

This is *the* place to hang out for under 21s. Watch the sunset with cool music playing as you enjoy some tasty pre-dinner snacks. Decide how you'll spend the next few days with your friends – old and new.

COOL CLUB

Home to some of the calmest, clearest blue seas in the area, we offer an incredible variety of activities, from windsurfing to sailing. Fly through the water powered by wind, engines, or your own power. Try something new or practise a sport that you love. Choose either morning or afternoon classes.

REMIX

Train to be a DJ on the coast. Every day we run two-hour courses teaching you how to mix songs and become familiar with the latest computer programs for concerts and dance events. If you're good enough, you may even be invited to make an appearance at our own club on Friday night!

BOOGIE!

Have you ever danced on a beach? Do you want to be more active! If so, come and learn new dance steps to great tunes every Wednesday afternoon. In the evening, we have fun dance events where you'll meet lots of people and practise what you've learned! A great experience for all!

OUT AND ABOUT

Join us from 7.00 am until the evening for a fascinating adventure away from the resort. Experience deep-sea fishing, swimming with dolphins and an afternoon tour through the spectacular mountains, where you'll see lots of birds and butterflies. A tasty lunch on a farm is included in the price.

2 Read again and answer the questions. Write the name of the activity.

Which activity allows you to
1 get fit and learn new dance skills to share with new friends? ....
2 try out a lot of different water sports? ....
3 have a competition with the people you know? ....
4 do a variety of very different activities in the same day? ....
5 challenge your body *and* your mind? ....
6 have the chance to show other people what you've learned, if you do well? ....
7 make plans for the rest of your holiday? ....
8 learn skills that other people will be able to enjoy later? ....

3 Match the highlighted words in the texts to the meanings.

1 where something is ....
2 extremely interesting ....
3 prove how good ....
4 certain to ....
5 being seen in public ....

1 Write full sentences using these words. Add any words you need.

0 Janet / need / pay attention / more / class
Janet needs to pay attention more in class.

1 If / you / go / France / should / buy / tourist guide

2 Look / sign! / We / have / remove / shoes

3 I / need / buy / more / paint / before / shop / closes

4 We / not / need / take / lunch tomorrow

5 You / should / not / take / photos / strangers

6 We / not / have / go / anywhere / tomorrow

2 One answer is not correct in each sentence. Choose the two correct answers.

0 If you have finished exercise 6 on page 7, you
   don't have to / needn't do any homework.
   a don't have to **b** shouldn't **c** needn't

1 You _____ buy your aunt a present;
   I've got something you can give her.
   a have to **b** needn't **c** don't have to

2 I _____ finish this now – can we chat later?
   a need to **b** have to **c** shouldn't

3 If you are feeling stressed, you
   _____ do some exercise. It really helps!
   a should **b** needn't **c** need to

4 Mark _____ go to football practice
   at 7.00 pm – everyone is expecting him.
   a shouldn't **b** has to **c** needs to

5 You _____ wait for me – I'll walk home on my own.
   a have to **b** don't have to **c** don't need to

3 Complete the email with modal verbs. Sometimes more than one answer is possible.

Hi Jessica,

I got your email last night about getting a visa to come and visit me in Australia. Firstly, you are right – you [1] _____ get a visa and you [2] _____ apply for that soon. You [3] _____ leave it until a few days before you go! You [4] _____ to worry about the cost because I'm going to pay for you. You [5] _____ put my address on the form as well because they need that information. You [6] _____ do anything else before you leave London, though, once you've got your visa.

See you very soon!

Sam

4 Complete the caption under each sign with a suitable modal verb.

HALF-PRICE FOR UNDER-15S

1 If you're under 15, you _____ pay the full price.

Entry for passengers only

2 You _____ enter here if you aren't a passenger.

GATE CLOSING IN 10 MINUTES →

3 You _____ get to the gate within the next ten minutes.

ALL LIBRARY BOOKS TO BE RETURNED BY END OF TERM

4 You _____ give your books back to the library before the end of term.

5 Complete the sentence with the correct form of *let* or *make*.

1 The guard _____ us show him our tickets before we could get on the train.

2 Airlines only _____ children travel alone if their parents complete a form.

3 My parents _____ me go on holiday with my friends when I was 16.

4 They _____ you listen to the safety announcement when you're on board a plane.

5 Jodie's mum and dad are _____ her start driving lessons soon.

6 The bus driver _____ us all sit down and fasten our seat belts.

6 Correct the mistakes in these sentences or put a tick (✓) by any you think are correct.

1 You don't bring any food, but please bring a football to the picnic.

2 You have to travel through the mountains to get to our house and the views are amazing.

3 You don't have to sit at a computer all day because it's bad for your eyes.

4 It's going to be sunny, so if you come, you should bring a sunhat.

1 Match the phrases with *on* to the meanings.

1 on board
2 on display
3 on foot
4 on purpose
5 on sale
6 on time
7 on my/your/his own

a not early or late
b alone
c on a boat, train or plane
d you can buy it
e walking somewhere
f arranged for people to look at
g intend to do something

2 Choose the correct answer.

1 I used to go to school *on foot / on time*, but now I take the bus.
2 The Year 12 art class have got their work *on purpose / on display* in the town library.
3 As soon as we were all *on time / on board*, they closed the doors of the plane.
4 I don't mind travelling *on board / on my own* because I always meet new people.
5 This mobile phone is only *on purpose / on sale* in this terminal!
6 It was an accident – I didn't do it *on my own / on purpose*.
7 The plane didn't leave *on time / on board* because there was a small engineering problem to fix.

1 Read this advertisement and complete the notes below it.

So you want to be a tour guide?

GenZ Travel Tours is looking for young, experienced travellers to guide groups of young teenagers around European cities. You should be a fun-loving, lively and responsible person with a university degree. We like our guides to speak at least one other language, in addition to English. This would be a fantastic first job for someone who loves travelling.

Send your CV by 30th March. For more information click <u>here</u>.

1 Job:
2 Qualifications:
3 Languages:
4 Personal characteristics:
5 Apply by:

🔊 06 **2 You will hear a woman called Lisa from a travel organisation for teens, talking about language exchange programmes. Listen and tick the things she mentions.**

a what an exchange is ☐
b where they will go ☐
c what they will do ☐
d what they will eat ☐
e what they will learn ☐
f who they will meet ☐

✓ PREPARE FOR THE EXAM

Listening Part 3

🔊 06 **3 Listen again. For each question, write the correct answer in the gap. Write one or two words or a number or a date or a time.**

TEEN TRAVEL: Language exchanges in Spain

Students experience what's known as a ^{1}'_____', and live with a family.
Most exchanges take place in ^{2}_____ time.
Students take part in activities, such as going for a meal or to the ^{3}_____.
Twice a week, Teen Travel organises events such as a ^{4}_____ or a visit.
^{5}_____ are not included in the price.
For more information contact Lisa ^{6}_____.

✓ EXAM TIPS

• You should only write one or two words, or a number, a date or a time.
• You can write numbers in figures or words.

VOCABULARY — Social media

1 Complete the crossword, using the clues below.

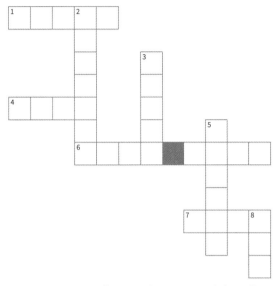

1 stop someone from seeing your social media page
2 write something, for example, your opinion
3 put someone else's message on your social media page, or a friend's social media page
4 show that you have read and that you approve of a message
5 choose to see everything that someone posts on social media
6 remove something so that it can't be seen any more
7 put something on a website or social media page
8 include someone using @ or their name

2 Choose the correct answer.

1 Megan *blocked / commented* on that video you put on your page.
2 I *shared / tagged* that article about teenagers with my friends.
3 Please will you *block / take down* that awful photo of me?
4 Do you *follow / like* Ed Sheeran on Twitter?
5 I'm going to *take down / block* Maggie – she always puts mean things online.
6 Jamie *posted / tagged* you in that photo we took at the party – it's really funny!
7 I loved that video of the cats you *posted / tagged* the other day!
8 Hardly anyone's *liked / commented* my latest post.

3 Complete the text with the words in the box.

block   comment   follow   like
post   share   tag   take down

I spend loads of time online. I don't like to miss out on what's happening out there! I update my status a few times every day and ¹ _____ stuff I think my friends will be interested in. I also like to ² _____ videos or articles I've found that I think people will like. Some are funny and some are serious. I like it when people ³ _____ on stuff I've posted. It's interesting to hear other people's opinions. I'm not bothered about whether people ⁴ _____' things – it's a bit lazy just to hit the button and not respond properly. Some people are only interested in getting 'likes' and put all kinds of rubbish online just to get a reaction. Who's really interested in what you had for lunch?! I don't ⁵ _____ my mates in photos without asking them first, and I ask people to ⁶ _____ stuff about me that I don't agree with. I don't ⁷ _____ any famous people like some of my friends do, but I do ⁸ _____ people whose attitudes and opinions I don't like.

4 Complete the speech bubbles in the cartoons. Use the correct form of some of the verbs from Exercise 3.

Oh, no! That's a horrible picture of me! Please _____ it _____.

That video of you is so funny! You should _____ it online and share it with all our friends.

I can't believe Andy put that horrible comment on my post. I'm going to _____ him.

Loads of people _____ my post. I think everyone agreed with what I said.

1 Read the title of the article below. What does it mean? Read the article quickly to find out.

IMPROVING IMAGES OR NOT?

Everybody knows that digital software is used to make images look different. The result of photoshopping? Models and celebrities are changed to look taller and younger; legs become thinner, skin becomes clearer, and hair becomes longer and thicker. There can be extreme edits, and few of those who are happy for their pictures to be photoshopped are likely to admit to it.

But there is a growing number of celebrities who are speaking out against photoshopping. American actor Jennifer Lawrence has made her opinions about it clear in public. She has talked about her body image and the demand to lose weight for her lead role in the hit film *The Hunger Games*. Her character, Katniss, doesn't have enough to eat, so of course the film-makers wanted Lawrence to look thin. The word is that J-Law refused to go on a diet for the part, and also insisted that clever photography should not be used to achieve a similar effect.

Rumer Willis has spoken about being treated unfairly by photographers after her image was altered following a shoot for a well-known magazine with her sisters Scout and Tallulah. The published photo showed that Rumer's jawline had been made smaller. Rumer did not appreciate this change and requested that anyone who had shared the picture online took it down. 'I love the way I look and I won't support anyone who would feel a need to change the way I look to make me more beautiful. Whether or not they realise it, it is a form of bullying, which I won't stand for,' she posted on her Instagram account.

Model Chrissy Teigen also had something to say about photoshopped images at the BeautyCon Festival in 2017. The festival celebrates natural beauty, and encourages people to be true to themselves. 'Nobody knows what a real face looks like any more,' said Chrissy. She also commented on society's unrealistic standards of beauty and how many photoshopped pictures there are on Instagram.

The message that many celebrities want to get out there is that people should learn to accept the way they look, even if it isn't 'perfect'. And it isn't just women who want to promote this idea. For his cover shoot for the American W magazine, actor Brad Pitt requested that his photo was not changed. Many more models and celebrities are starting to express similar opinions and disagreeing with the use of photo techniques that produce impossible images. It looks like this is the beginning of a new generation of responsible celebrities.

2 Read the article again and the questions below. For each question, choose A, B, C or D.

1 In the second paragraph, the writer is
- **A** supporting Jennifer Lawrence's point of view about photoshopping.
- **B** describing what Jennifer Lawrence did to prepare for a film role.
- **C** explaining Jenifer Lawrence's attitude towards being filmed.
- **D** encouraging readers to follow Jennifer Lawrence's actions.

2 In the paragraph about Rumer Willis, we find out that
- **A** she did not have a problem with her appearance.
- **B** she wrote to the magazine to complain about the photo they took.
- **C** she did not agree with how photographers behaved towards her sisters.
- **D** she made sure that she blocked her photo from her followers on Instagram.

3 What does the writer say is the aim of the BeautyCon Festival?
- **A** to allow beauty experts to give their opinions
- **B** to discuss the best ways of photographing people
- **C** to make people feel more confident in the way they look
- **D** to try to ban photoshopped images from social media sites

4 What point does the writer make about celebrities in the final paragraph?
- **A** They want to find new methods of photography.
- **B** They are changing opinions about what beauty is.
- **C** They want the beauty industry to stop using models.
- **D** They are in a good position to change people's minds.

5 Which of these would make a good alternative title for the article?
- **A** Celebrities support actors who are not respected by the media.
- **B** Celebrities refuse to have their photos in magazines.
- **C** Celebrities give their opinions on what real beauty is.
- **D** Celebrities are changing the photography industry.

EXAM TIPS
- Identify the key words in the questions first.
- When you have chosen your answer, check again with the text.

1 Write the words in the correct order to make passive sentences.

1 computer / My / fixed / by / my / was / friend

2 films / A lot of / watched / laptops / on / are

3 an / prize / won / 11-year-old boy / The / was / by

4 stories / by / Most children / their / are / parents / read

5 computer / in the 1950s / first / invented / The / was / personal

6 injured / busy / Two / that / road / on / teenagers / were

2 Choose the correct answer.

1 You shouldn't *take / be taken* photos of people without asking their permission.
2 You *might / can* be surprised by how good the photos are when you see them.
3 *Bicycles must ride / Bicycles must be ridden* on the special path.
4 *People must warn / People must be warned* that the beach isn't clean.
5 Under-18s *may use / may be used* this club.
6 Many apps *can download / can be downloaded* for free.

3 Complete the modal passives with the verbs in the box.

change	improve	make
predict	upload	~~use~~

Digital editing software can often ⁰ *be used* to change your appearance on screen. For example, your skin could easily ¹ _____ to remove spots; the colour of your eyes could even ² _____ from blue to brown. The final images can then ³ _____ to a social networking site. So, how can we ever be sure that something posted online is real? Does that matter? Is it only natural for people to want to look good and therefore every effort must ⁴ _____ to achieve the perfect end result? Given the speed at which 3D technology is developing, future possibilities in this area can't ⁵ _____ . What do *you* think?

4 Complete the article about the British Library.

The world's BIGGEST library

The British Library in the UK has the largest number of items in the world. It ¹ _____ (create) in 1973 and its collections ² _____ (base) on things which ³ _____ (give) to the British Museum (which the library was once part of) along with other things it gained. For a long time the library's books and other items ⁴ _____ (hold) in different buildings around London, before moving to a new building which ⁵ _____ (build) especially for the library. However, some items have since ⁶ _____ (move) to another centre in the north of England, where over seven million of the library's 174 million-plus items ⁷ _____ (keep).

5 Correct the mistakes in these sentences or put a tick (✓) by any you think are correct.

1 The photos were taken in a beautiful park.

2 This game it's can be played online.

3 My best friend called Julia.

4 The food was tasted horrible, but I ate it.

5 I saw a school that made of wood.

6 I was given this phone for my birthday.

VOCABULARY Phrases with *in*

1 Write the letters in the correct order to make phrases with *in*.

1 VANCEDA in
2 EFUTUR in
3 LEGNEAR in
4 RIARPUCALT in
5 HET DEN in
6 CFAT in
7 LEADTI in

2 Complete the sentences with a phrase from Exercise 1.

1 You should let the teacher know _____ if you are unable to go on the school trip.
2 Read the application form _____ – you don't want to miss anything.
3 All the dresses are lovely, but I like the red dress _____ .
4 _____ everyone agreed on the party theme, but it wasn't easy.
5 _____ the weather in southern Europe is warmer all year than it is here.
6 Mercedes loved everything about the holiday: _____ she said it was the best ever!
7 _____ it would be better if you did your work on the computer. I can't read your writing.

WRITING An online review

≫ See *Prepare to write* box, Student's Book page 79.

1 Read these questions and choose the best answer for you.

1 Do you take lots of photographs?
   a yes, all the time
   b sometimes
   c hardly at all
2 How do you take photos?
   a with my phone
   b with a camera
   c with both
3 What do you mainly take photos of?
   a myself
   b my friends
   c other things
4 Do you share your photos?
   a yes – on social media all the time
   b from time to time – if there's a really good picture
   c not really – they're for me

2 Which of these words and phrases could you use in a positive review? Which would you use in a negative review? Add them to the table.

awesome	amazing	disappointing
limited	not worth …	one advantage
the disadvantage is …		too expensive

Positive	Negative

3 Write a review of a website which people can upload photos to.

Say:
one thing that is good about it
one thing that could be improved
whether you would recommend the website to other people

14 LET'S COOK!

1 Look at the picture and complete the text with suitable verbs in the correct form.

In the picture we can see two teenagers preparing dinner. The boy is ¹ _____ some tomatoes in a pan on the cooker, and he's ² _____ them all the time. There's a kettle next to him, which is ³ _____. In the oven we can see a chicken, which is ⁴ _____. He's also preparing some toast in the toaster, but it's ⁵ _____! Outside, his sister is ⁶ _____ some meat. Their friends are going to arrive very soon.

2 Choose the two correct verbs in each list.

1 You do this with a spoon.	taste	stir	burn
2 A way of cooking meat.	barbecue	bite	roast
3 You do this with your mouth.	bite	fry	taste
4 You do this over heat.	boil	taste	fry
5 Something you can do to bread.	burn	bake	boil
6 You can do this to vegetables with water.	steam	fry	boil
7 You can do this with oil.	fry	roast	freeze
8 A way of cooking fish.	grill	taste	fry

3 Choose the correct answer.

1 Would you like to *bite / taste* this to see if there's enough salt?

2 Every Sunday we *roast / stir* a piece of meat for lunch.

3 I want you to *steam / stir* this sauce for me – don't stop!

4 Can you *boil / barbecue* some water for me, please?

5 Many people like the sound of *grilling / biting* into an apple.

6 Watch the pan and don't let the onions *freeze / burn*.

7 The first thing to do is to *fry / bake* some vegetables in a pan.

8 I'm hungry – we should *freeze / barbecue* these sausages now.

4 Complete the instructions with the words in the box.

bite	boil	burn	freeze
fry	stir	taste	

How to make spaghetti bolognese

1 _____ the onion and garlic together and add some tomatoes.

2 Fill a saucepan with water, add some salt and _____.

3 Add some beef to the onion and tomato mixture and _____ without stopping, so that it doesn't _____. Then get a spoon and _____ a little to make sure it's delicious!

4 Add the pasta to the water. When you think it is cooked, _____ into it to see if it is ready.

5 If you have made plenty of sauce, you can even _____ some so you can eat it later!

1 Look at the texts quickly. What kind of texts are they?

0
Fry onions and peppers in a little oil. Add the sauce mix from the bottle and stir. Pour over meat or fish for a tasty dish!

1
From: Sam:
Dad – shall we organise a surprise dinner for Mum? I'm at the supermarket now. I could get a chicken to roast and you could boil some potatoes. What do you think?

2
Safety instructions
Steam cooker gets extremely hot. Keep dry cloths near for when handling items to prevent burns. Open door carefully and stand away from steam. Do not open door while in use.

3

To: Simon   Reply Forward
From: Harry's café

Thank you for applying for the waiter's job. We are pleased to invite you for an interview on Monday 12th April at 3.30 pm. Let us know, if you are not able to attend.

4
Hey Nicholas!
Having an amazing time in Greece, working at a restaurant by the harbour. It's like being on holiday! They need a new chef in the kitchen – why don't you apply?
Alex

5
From: Carolina:
Mandi! You're coming to my party tomorrow, right? Can you bring something to barbecue? There are plenty of burgers, but no sausages or vegetables. See you at 1.30!

PREPARE FOR THE EXAM

Reading Part 1

2 Look at the text in each question. What does it say? Choose A, B or C.

0 Example:
   A This recipe is for vegetarians.
   B The sauce bottle contains vegetables.
   C The sauce can be added to other food.

1 A Sam's mother does not know what Dad and Sam are planning.
   B Sam can cook chicken but doesn't know how to cook potatoes.
   C Sam and his Dad have already arranged to cook dinner for Sam's mum.

2 The instructions suggest that
   A the door will not open when food is cooking.
   B steam may escape from items in the cooker.
   C using the cooker can be dangerous.

3 Simon should
   A contact the café if he wants information about a job.
   B start work at the café on Monday afternoon.
   C say whether he can go to the interview.

4 A Alex wants to get a job where Nicholas works.
   B Alex wants Nicholas to join him in Greece.
   C Nicholas is coming to Greece for a holiday.

5 A Carolina wants Mandi to do something.
   B There won't be much food to eat at the party.
   C Carolina doesn't know if Mandi is going to the party.

EXAM TIPS

- In this part of the test you have to read five short messages, which may be notes, postcards, emails, messages, labels, signs and so on.
- You need to think about the main message of the text before choosing your answer.

3 Match the **highlighted** words in the texts to the meanings.

1 a piece of material ....
2 make a liquid flow from or into a container ....
3 stop something happening ....
4 put something with something else ....
5 go to ....

1 Complete the relative clauses with *who, which* or *whose.*

1 Food websites, _____ often have easy recipes, are becoming very popular.
2 My best friend, _____ love of food is well-known, always takes photos of her meals.
3 Chef Martha Webster, _____ is talking on TV at the moment, has her own website.
4 This cookbook, _____ contains traditional recipes, was given to me by my grandmother.
5 Italy, _____ food is just delicious, is where my parents are from.
6 Green smoothies, _____ contain vegetables, are becoming popular.

2 Complete the sentences with the correct phrases below. Use *which, who* or *whose* to make a single sentence.

> has just gone to university
> methods are actually quite hard
> my grandmother always made for me
> I had bought the day before
> husband makes wonderful meals
> is closed on Sundays
> ~~uses local produce~~

0 The restaurant near my house, *which uses local produce* , makes excellent pasta dishes.
1 My mum's best friend, _____ , has invited me to dinner.
2 This Australian Christmas cookbook, _____ , is really a collection of summer recipes.
3 The shop near my house, _____ , is running a special offer on sugar-free drinks.
4 My favourite dessert, _____ , has apples and cinnamon in it.
5 Jack chose a piece of fruit, _____ , to put in his lunchbox.
6 Julia's older sister, _____ , has found a part-time job in an expensive restaurant.

3 These sentences contain defining or non-defining relative clauses. Add commas where necessary to show the three non-defining relative clauses.

1 The book that I started reading at the weekend is really difficult.
2 My Auntie Maria who lives in Spain is a lawyer.
3 We're staying at the La Vida resort which Mum's friend recommended to us.
4 The man who lives across the street from my friend is a teacher.
5 The boy who is holding the ball is my cousin.
6 Darcie showed me a photo of her sister who is a ballet dancer.

4 Complete the article about a celebrity chef with *where, who, whose, that* or *which.*

Celebrity chefs are not uncommon, but Andy Perez, [1] _____ grew up in San Diego, California, is a little different to most. By the time he was 9, he could chop vegetables as quickly as the kitchen staff at his parents' restaurant, and when he left school, he was working in several restaurants [2] _____ he learned to cook healthy, delicious meals.

While he was working at one restaurant, [3] _____ was called The Boathouse, the young chef appeared in a TV documentary about it. A TV production company then asked him to make his own programme, called *Andy's Kitchen*. After the series, [4] _____ was a huge success, Andy published a cookbook with the same name. It was bought by people [5] _____ were of different age groups and it became a number 1 bestseller.

Since then, Andy, [6] _____ aim is to get people eating healthier food, has been involved in many other projects. One of these included going into schools [7] _____ serve lunch for their students, and introducing the idea of healthier meals for children. Andy is now one of the most successful TV chefs in the USA, and he owns several restaurants [8] _____ are popular throughout the country.

5 Correct the mistakes in these sentences or put a tick (✓) by any you think are correct.

1 There I met Jack, is a very funny boy.
_____

2 We can visit São Paulo, where has a lot of great restaurants.
_____

3 It's about an astronaut, whose spaceship gets attacked by aliens.
_____

4 Some new friends were sitting around the table were very friendly.
_____

5 I have a friend which is called Manuel.
_____

1 Tick (✓) the sentences which contain transitive verbs.

1 This sauce tastes delicious! ☐
2 Dad barbecued some chicken. ☐
3 The bread is baking in the oven. ☐
4 I'm going to steam the vegetables. ☐
5 The onions are frying in butter. ☐
6 Can I have a piece of that cake? ☐

2 Look at the pairs of sentences. Which one is transitive? Which one is intransitive? Write T or I.

1 a Shall we grill some seafood over the fire? ....
  b Is that meat grilled? ....
2 a I don't know whether to boil the beef or fry it. ....
  b The water's boiling now. ....
3 a Wow! This pasta tastes amazing! ....
  b Can I taste your dessert? ....

LISTENING

1 Look at the pictures below. What does each one show?

✓ PREPARE FOR THE EXAM

Listening Part 1

2 Listen and choose the correct answer for each question.

1 How will the man cook the lamb?

5 What does the woman enjoy baking?

2 What does the girl decide to have for lunch?

6 Where will they go to get mushrooms?

3 What food does the new restaurant serve?

7 Which ingredients will the boy use for dinner?

4 What will they do in the park?

✓ EXAM TIPS

- Read the questions carefully and underline important words.
- Check all your answers when you listen for the second time.

15 CITY OR COUNTRY?

VOCABULARY — Artificial and natural world

1 **Match the words to their meanings.**

1 valley ....
2 wildlife ....
3 bugs ....
4 ruin ....
5 pollution ....
6 facilities ....
7 seasons ....
8 health centre ....

a the damaged parts of an old building
b insects
c the buildings, equipment and services provided for a particular purpose
d a place, sometimes part of a hospital, to go for medical treatment or advice
e an area of low land between hills or mountains, often with a river
f the four periods of the year, each lasting around three months
g animals and plants growing independently of people in their natural environment
h damage caused to water, air, etc. by harmful substances or waste

2 **Complete 1–5 with the words in the box to make phrases.**

architecture   buildings   conditioning
lights   spaces

1 historic ....
2 open ....
3 air ....
4 street ....
5 modern ....

3 **Complete the sentences with the phrases from Exercise 2.**

1 When it gets really hot, we turn on the ....
2 I really like the way this town is set out because there are plenty of .... to walk and relax in.
3 If you go to the countryside, you'll see lots of stars because there aren't any ....
4 Some people really dislike .... because they say that it doesn't fit in with the older buildings.
5 If you want to see .... in Sydney, you should visit the Old Post Office and Central Railway Station.

4 **Choose the correct answers.**

1 I love going on holiday to interesting places in the summer. It's true that if you go to a city, there's *pollution / seasons* because of the cars, which is worse when it's hot, and if you visit the countryside, there might be *bugs / seasons*. But summer's still the best time of year to go away. Paris is my favourite city because I love the mix of *modern architecture / wildlife* and *historic buildings / valleys*.
2 I live in Switzerland and most people think of how lovely the mountains are, but down in the *ruins / valleys* it is just as beautiful. You can see lots of *facilities / wildlife* such as mountain rabbits, especially in the *open spaces / historic buildings*. At night we have a great view of the stars because there aren't any *street lights / facilities*.
3 Last year my family and I went to Egypt on holiday. We visited the pyramids and the ancient *ruins / centres*. I loved Cairo because there are lots of *facilities / seasons* there for young people. It was summer though – the hottest *pollution / season*! I was glad our hotel had *air conditioning / facilities*.

1 Read the article below quickly. Where does Phil live? What has he just done?

2 Read the article again and answer the questions. Choose the correct answer.

My first visit to the city

by Phil Jenkins

I've just returned from spending a week in the city with my cousin, Jed. I live with my parents and sister in a small country village, so it was interesting to go and find out about city life.

The first thing I noticed was the cost of everything. Cities are really expensive, and we spent loads when we ate out in a café. Every day, we went into the city centre, but because Jed lives a 30-minute train ride out of town, it was easier to stay in the city than go back to eat. Luckily, Jed knew some cheaper takeaway places that did stuff like salads and vegetable soups. They're not things I'd usually choose – burgers are more my thing – but I tried a lot of new things and I found quite a few vegetables and things that I actually liked – Mum'll be pleased I'm sure!

I missed the peace and quiet of the countryside a little, though the city traffic didn't bother me. I saw some amazing fast cars I've never seen in the countryside. I soon got used to being among all the people, too. City life's got a real buzz about it! I met all Jed's friends and noticed that they were wearing expensive clothes with logos. At first, I felt a bit uncomfortable in my own stuff – just old jeans and shirts I wear round the farm – but then my cousin lent me these really stylish trainers which made me feel like I fitted in with the crowd a bit better! But it didn't really matter. I saw all kinds of people wearing all kinds of things and I liked the fact that in the city you can wear whatever you want.

After a few days, I started to run out of money, so we had to find other things to do rather than shopping or eating out. I was amazed by how many free or cheap things there are to do in a city. For example, one lunchtime we walked into a museum where a really cool band was playing. You'd never get that in our little village museum! There were loads of other things I didn't get to do in the city – but that just means there's more for next time.

Before I went to the city, I'd always thought of myself as a country boy. I love going out riding, helping on my dad's farm and having an outdoor life. Now I've seen what else is available, I might want to spend more of my time in the city. I guess the ideal thing would be to get a flat and work in the city when I'm old enough, but escape to the country at the weekend. Then I'd get the best of both worlds – can't wait!

1 What is the main point of the article?
  A to give advice about things to do in the city
  B to compare living in the city with the countryside
  C to warn readers about how expensive city living is
  D to describe someone's feelings about an experience
2 What does Phil say about eating in the city?
  A They had burgers and other fast food.
  B They bought a range of healthy foods.
  C They wanted to eat in expensive restaurants.
  D They preferred taking the train home for lunch.
3 During his time in the city, Phil felt
  A nervous about meeting new people.
  B annoyed by all the traffic noise.
  C embarrassed about his sense of style.
  D bothered by the crowds.

4 How does Phil feel about the city?
  A surprised by the range of things there was to do there
  B excited about going back to visit as soon as he can
  C unsure about whether he wants to live there
  D disappointed that he didn't get to see everything
5 What email would Phil send to his cousin Jed?
  A I really enjoyed staying with you, but I definitely prefer being in the countryside.
  B You never know, one day I might come and live in the city – maybe we could share an apartment!
  C I haven't made up my mind whether I prefer the city or the country, but I had a brilliant time with you!
  D I found the city a bit scary, so I'm really glad I had you to show me around!

1 Complete the sentences with *a/an, the* or – (zero article).

1 Stuart is _____ car mechanic at _____ local garage.

2 _____ Statue of Liberty is in New York.

3 _____ happiness doesn't come from _____ money.

4 Have you ever visited _____ capital of Sweden? It's beautiful.

5 Call _____ fire station! There's _____ fire!

6 I love these shoes. Are they made of _____ leather?

7 There's _____ mouse on _____ table in _____ kitchen.

8 Nobody saw _____ shark as it swam past _____ boat.

2 Add articles to this text where necessary.

My mum is a waitress in restaurant in city about 20 km from our home. She has worked at restaurant for 15 years, but she wants to be teacher. At the moment, she is studying at university in our town. She never complains about all work she has to do. When she finishes university, we're going to visit USA. Then, I think she'll decide on next course she wants to do!

3 Read the fact file and decide which articles are correct. Correct the incorrect ones.

COUNTRY FEATURE – NEW ZEALAND

The country of New Zealand is in the south-western Pacific Ocean. The country is made up of the islands, and it is called island country. It is situated about 1500 km east of Australia and about 1000 km south of the Pacific islands of New Caledonia, Fiji and Tonga. It is a long way from anywhere!

People in New Zealand speak the English and Maori. A capital of New Zealand is the Wellington. New Zealand is famous for many things, including its beautiful scenery, which is made up of the mountains, the beaches and the volcanoes. There are many species of bird that can only be found in New Zealand, including birds which cannot fly.

Do you know anything else about this country, which is so far from anywhere? Write to us at **countrieswelove@travelteens.uk**

PREPARE FOR THE EXAM

Reading Part 6

4 Read the article below and think of the word which best fits each gap. Use only one word in each gap. There is an example at the beginning.

SPENDING TIME OUTDOORS

Do you live in a city or ⁰ *the* countryside? With ¹ _____ holidays coming up soon, will you get outdoors or sit inside in front of ² _____ screen? British adventurer Ben Fogle has spoken about worries that young people in the UK spend too much time indoors. ³ _____ online survey showed that only a third of parents had taken their kids to look at ⁴ _____ stars or to go fishing, for example. ⁵ _____ same survey also found that only a third of parents had gone for ⁶ _____ walk in the hills with their children. Fogle said, 'Because of issues from ⁷ _____ computer games to a lack of local green spaces, we have lost our sense of adventure, a little, as a nation.'

EXAM TIPS

- Read the whole text first for meaning.
- Look at the gaps and think about what the missing words could be.
- Write your answers and then check again by reading through the whole text.

5 Choose the correct sentence in each pair.

1 a We went to cinema on Saturday to see a film.
  b We went to the cinema on Saturday to see a film.

2 a Did you see the news last night?
  b Did you see a news last night?

3 a Do you have time in next week to meet up?
  b Do you have time in the next week to meet up?

4 a I would advise you to do the same as me.
  b I would advise you to do same as me.

5 a That was a best restaurant I've ever been to.
  b That was the best restaurant I've ever been to.

VOCABULARY — Phrasal verbs

1 Write the letters in the correct order to make verbs.

1 owhs ....
2 ayts ....
3 chact ....
4 den ....
5 emvo ....

2 Complete the sentences with a verb from Exercise 1 and a preposition from the box below. You need to use one verb twice.

> around   in (x2)   out   up (x2)

1 I haven't seen Becky for a long time – I must .... with her soon.
2 Tess had found an apartment and .... on Saturday.
3 I think I'll .... this weekend and do all that biology homework.
4 After the film, we went to Mickey's house and .... watching another film because we couldn't think of anything else to do!
5 It was my first visit to London and my cousin .... me .... the city.
6 My brother doesn't like his housemates and so he wants to ....

WRITING — An email (2)

>> See *Prepare to write* box, Student's Book page 89.

1 Complete the sentences with the words in the box.

> actually   despite   finally   however

1 We went down to the beach .... the rain. You get wet in the sea anyway!
2 It took us ages to bring the cows home, but we .... managed it.
3 People think living in the countryside's boring but, ..., there's plenty to do.
4 The journey through the mountains was amazing. Unfortunately, ..., the family next to us was really noisy!
5 I've .... managed to get us tickets for that concert you wanted to go to.
6 .... being in a huge apartment block, my flat is really quiet.
7 I would love to visit the city. ...., I would need someone to show me around.
8 People think I'm a city person, but .... I love spending time in the countryside, too.

2 Read the email below and Sam's reply. Then answer the questions.

From: Jem
Subject: This weekend

Hi!
Good news! I can come and visit you this weekend! — Great!
I've never been to the countryside before. Is there anything in particular I should bring? — Tell Jem
What are we going to do while I'm there? Can we go walking or will we help your dad on the farm? — Say what
You said there was a concert in the village on Sunday night. Shall we go? — No, because …
See you soon!
Jem

Hi Jem!
It's great news that you can come and visit me this weekend!
Bring some walking boots with you because it can be muddy around the farm. However, I think it's going to be hot on Sunday, so bring your shorts as well.
Working on the farm's really interesting, so let's do that. You can feed the cows and we can help Dad mend some fences. Does that sound OK to you?
We can't go to the concert, actually, because it's been cancelled. They didn't sell enough tickets! We can watch a film instead.
I can't wait to show you around!
Sam

Does Sam
use linking words to link his ideas?
use adjectives to make his writing more interesting?
use informal language and short forms?

PREPARE FOR THE EXAM

Writing Part 1

3 Now write your answer to Jem's email. Use different ideas to Sam. Don't forget to use linking words, adjectives, informal language and short forms. Write about 100 words.

EXAM TIPS

- Make sure you develop the ideas in your email.
- Use paragraphs to introduce new ideas.

VOCABULARY Film

1 Complete the crossword, using the clues on the right.

1 when you act, dance, sing or play music to entertain people
2 tell the people in a film what to do
3 an actor's part in a film or play
4 speech or music that is on a CD or sound file
5 the person who tells the people in a film what to do
6 made with moving drawings, not real people or animals
7 when a film becomes available to see
8 be in a play or film
9 a film or play with singing and dancing
10 the music used in a film or a TV show

2 Write the words in the correct column. Some may go into the table twice.

animated   appear   come out   direct   director   musical
performance   recording   role   soundtrack

	Verb	Noun	Adjective
Music/Theatre			
Film			

3 Complete the text with words from Exercise 2.

Last month, the school drama group produced a play. Mr Simms, our drama teacher, was the ¹_____ and he was great – very patient with the actors! He held some classes, where we learned to act, and I was really pleased when he gave me the lead ²_____. Most of my friends ³_____ in the play, too. It was a ⁴_____, so there were songs as well. We were all a bit nervous about singing in front of people, but our music teacher made a ⁵_____ during one of our singing practices and when we listened to it, we realised it sounded pretty good, so we felt less worried. We had several ⁶_____ of the play and it was a huge success!

1 The people below all want to do a course. What kind of course do they each want to do?

1 **Alison** and her grandmother Nell both love working with cameras and computers, and want to do a course together every weekend. Nell can drive them to different locations.

2 **Jasmine** loves working on school plays and wants to learn more about technical things in the theatre. She needs a course at weekends, where she can help on a local project.

3 **Artur** wants to improve the design of his blog and add some stylish effects. He'd like a course lasting a few hours, with additional practice to take away with him.

4 **Gabby** wants to invite her best friend on a full-day course as a present. They enjoy anything about clothes and personal appearance. Gabby wants to have a nice meal afterwards, too.

5 **Nelson** wants to learn about developing online games on an evening course. He'd like to add music and animation to his own games site.

2 Here are eight advertisements for courses. Decide which course would be the most suitable for the people in Exercise 1.

A Perform
Learn how to set up lights for a performance. We look at different positions for lights and their special effects, including the use of colour. During the course, you'll design and build the lighting for the town's summer show. There are ten weekly classes on Saturday mornings.

B Create
This course on Mondays (18.30–20.30) is for anyone who wants to explore their creative skills digitally, especially those who enjoy internet gaming. We look at 3D techniques, cartoon drawing, and how to make a model and bring it to life. There's also an opportunity to learn about music and video editing.

C Be a star
Do you enjoy performing in school plays? This weekend course provides practical tips for future careers in the theatre or television, and helps you prepare for that important first role. This is a weekend course for anyone who wants to be a star! Meals and refreshments are included in the course fee.

D Images
Learn how to improve your photography or turn your old family albums into amazing digital books with easy-to-use software. The course includes some trips to beautiful places, where you'll get expert advice on taking better pictures. It is open to all ages and takes place on Saturdays over eight weeks.

E Online 2
This course continues from Online 1 and in the same way it offers excellent support material to work on at home, following this half-day Saturday class. Building a website and communicating online isn't difficult these days – but we can direct you in making improvements to your website or online space, with help on technical things.

F Design and play
Do you love playing computer games? Do you have ideas for your own games? If the answer to these questions is yes, then this course is for you. It runs two afternoons a week during the school holidays. You'll leave with a game designed by you!

G Get practical
You must have your own digital camera and be an experienced photographer to attend this practical evening course. Learn how to take high-quality photos of items such as clothes and make-up, for use online. Afterwards, you may even be ready to earn some money!

H Style time
Do you know what looks good on you? Do you know how to choose the right make-up and hairstyle? In this fun Saturday workshop, you'll get answers to all these questions, and more. We also offer celebration lunches if you're here for a special occasion! Discounts available for two or more people.

3 Match the highlighted words and phrases in the advertisements to the meanings.

1 think about something in order to find out more about it
2 relating to experiences or real situations rather than ideas or imagination
3 what you need for a particular activity
4 images in a film which seem real but are created by artists and technical experts
5 make changes to a film, deciding what will be removed or kept in

GRAMMAR Reported speech

1 Write the words in the correct order to complete the sentences.

1 Jack said … (was / directing / a / that / new film / he)
Jack said _____.

2 Amy said … (new film / just / out / her / had / come)
Amy said _____.

3 The newspapers said … (performance / the young actor / had / amazing / given / an)
The newspapers said _____.

4 He said … (each day / would / they / films / two / show)
He said _____.

5 The actor said … (more questions / could / that / he / answer / later)
The actor said _____.

6 He said … (surprise / to hand out / gifts / had / some / also / he)
He said _____.

2 You have a new 'e-friend' called Ana and you Skyped for the first time yesterday. Here are some things that Ana said to you. Now tell another friend what Ana said.

0 I live in a small village with my parents.
Ana said she lived in a small village with her parents.

1 In my free time I do aerial yoga.
She said that _____

2 I'm learning two foreign languages at the moment, including Chinese.
_____

3 I hope I can visit you next year.
_____

4 I haven't visited an English-speaking country before.
_____

5 I can play three musical instruments including the piano.
_____

6 I'll send you a short video of my band soon.
_____

3 Your friend says some things that are different from what she said before. Correct her, using the information in brackets.

0 We're going to the cinema on Saturday evening. (afternoon)
Really? You said *we were going on Saturday afternoon.*

1 We're having pizza for dinner tonight. (sausages and potatoes)
Are we? You said _____.

2 I borrowed a book from the library yesterday. (last week)
Did you? You said _____.

3 My uncle doesn't like going to the cinema in the afternoon. (loved it)
Really? You said _____.

4 My aunt will pick me up after football tomorrow. (dance class / Saturday)
Really? You said _____.

5 Our friend Georgia has directed a short film. (acted in)
Really? You said _____.

6 Jack has just uploaded his new film to YouTube. (uploaded / five weeks ago)
Really? You said _____.

4 Correct the mistakes in these sentences or put a tick (✓) by any you think are correct.

1 I told my friend about a wildlife programme I've seen on TV.
_____

2 She said me that she loved it very much.
_____

3 The next month I received a call saying that I needed to go and register.
_____

4 I asked she to send me the photo she had taken.
_____

5 He said that he will help us expand our knowledge about things that are taking place around us.
_____

Reporting verbs

1 Match the reporting verbs to their meanings.

1 insist
2 announce
3 demand
4 explain
5 suggest

a make something clear to understand by giving details

b express a plan or idea for someone to consider

c tell people something officially

d say firmly that something must be done

e ask for something in a way that shows you do not expect to be refused

2 You heard this conversation in a gaming store. Complete the text below, reporting the conversation with the correct form of the verbs in the box.

Marty: Hello, I bought this video game last week but I'd like to return it, please.

Manager: Sure. What's the problem?

Marty: It doesn't work properly. It keeps stopping.

Manager: OK. Sorry about that. Have you got the receipt?

Marty: No, I haven't.

Manager: I do need to see the receipt, I'm afraid, or I won't be able to help.

Marty: That's the problem – I've lost it.

Manager: I'm sorry but there isn't much I can do to help in that case.

Marty: I'm not very happy with that. I'd like to talk to someone else then.

Manager: I'm sorry but there isn't anyone else here. Why don't you contact our head office?

> demand   explain   insist
> say   suggest   tell

Marty ¹ _____ that he had a game he wanted to return. He ² _____ that it didn't work properly. The manager ³ _____ that Marty show him the receipt. Marty ⁴ _____ him that he couldn't show him the receipt because he had lost it. The manager apologised and said he couldn't help Marty, so Marty ⁵ _____ that he talk to someone else. The manager was on his own and ⁶ _____ that Marty could contact head office.

1 You are going to hear six conversations. Read the questions below. What topics link the questions?

 PREPARE FOR THE EXAM

Listening Part 2

2 For each question, choose the correct answer. Then listen again and check your answers.

08

1 You will hear two friends talking about making a video clip for a competition.
The boy says that he is unsure about
A whether he will include a soundtrack.
B the filming techniques he will use.
C the topic of his clip.

2 You will hear two students talking about their acting class.
What do they agree about?
A how patient the teacher is
B how amusing the classes are
C how interesting the activities are

3 You will hear two friends talking about a musical film they have seen.
What did they both like about it?
A the soundtrack
B the acting
C the special effects

4 You will hear two friends talking about getting a place at drama school.
How does the girl feel now?
A confident that her friend will be accepted
B pleased by how well her interview went
C surprised that they haven't heard about it yet

5 You will hear two students talking about a camera skills class.
The girl says that she
A found it difficult to manage her time.
B found the subject matter very interesting.
C found it hard to understand the teacher's instructions.

6 You will hear two friends talking about actors.
What does the boy say about them?
A They are paid too much.
B They do nothing useful.
C They have some strange ideas.

EXAM TIPS

- You may have to answer questions about how someone is feeling, or what they think about something. Listen carefully for meaning.
- Remember that you hear each conversation twice. Check your answers when you hear the recording a second time.

VOCABULARY — Verbs of communication

1 Write the letters in the correct order to make words.

1 esigolpoa ....
2 rimden ....
3 wran ....
4 kejo ....
5 rewnod ....
6 eegiards ....
7 caplimon ....
8 misrope ....

2 Choose the correct answer.

1 Jake *apologised / promised* for calling at midnight.
2 Mum is always *complaining / apologising* about the time I spend on social media.
3 Martine and I *wondered / joked* about photos of her as a baby. They were so funny!
4 Can you *disagree / remind* me to email you this photo of us when I get home?
5 Everyone in my class *joked / disagreed* with my opinion of the book.
6 I hate biology and I'm *wondering / warning* if I made the right subject choices last year.
7 Your sister *apologised / promised* to give me back the money I lent her last week.
8 The teachers *warned / complained to* us about the dangers of social media.

3 Complete the text with the correct form of the verbs from Exercise 1.

4 Look at the cartoons and complete the captions with the correct verbs from Exercise 1.

I .... you! It's going to rain – please take the umbrella!

I .... to love you forever.

I'm texting to .... because I can't come to your house later. We're going shopping.

I .... whether I'll have time to play football today. I hope so!

Yesterday, I was studying when Mum ¹ .... me that our favourite TV programme was on. It's about teenager and parent stuff and last night's was about social media. First, they showed a story of a lonely boy called Kyle, who ² .... whether he would ever have any friends. Two boys in his class ³ .... about him online, but it wasn't funny to him. In the end, one of the boys ⁴ ...., but it was too late – Kyle had lost his self-confidence.

The programme also ⁵ .... us to be careful about the people you talk to on social media. Sometimes, you don't know them and they might be dangerous. The next part was interesting. So, many parents ⁶ .... about their kids using social media, telling them to turn their phone off at the table and so on. The film showed a mother, who had no idea her daughter had friends all across the world and she saw the positive side of social media! It's a great programme to watch with a parent because you will certainly ⁷ .... about some things, and you can have a good discussion about them. Last night's programme was interesting and I ⁸ .... Mum I'd be more open about my online use in case there were ever any problems.

READING

1 Look at the texts quickly. What kind of texts are they?

0

To: Rosie
From:

I'm glad you came to stay at the weekend! I feel bad that you couldn't sleep because my room's noisy, though – it's all the traffic outside. We'll use my sister's room next time.

Maggie

1

Competition!

Win a phone: complete the form and send it.

Win an amazing range of apps, too!

Open to people aged 16+ only.

2

Send a message in a bottle from Chesil Beach! Write an interesting note and wait for a reply from somewhere exciting!

3

Jen says: You know it's my birthday soon? Well, I want to celebrate with you all! Be at my place 2pm Sunday. No presents, just bring something to put on the barbecue!

4

Max, I've left my phone on the kitchen table. You've got a talent for technology – can you find out why it won't send texts? Thanks! See you after school. Meg

5

Hey Charlotte! Fancy coming to a sign language class with me? We can learn how to communicate with some of our deaf friends. There'll be loads to learn, but it sounds fun and we can practise together after classes! Pixie

Reading Part 1

2 **What does each text say? Choose A, B or C.**

0 Maggie is writing to
  A complain about something.
  B apologise for something.
  C thank someone.

1 **A** Not everyone can enter this competition.
  B To win the competition, you must ask for a form.
  C There are prizes for two different winners.

2 People who send a message in a bottle
  A must wait for the answer on Chisel Beach.
  B must not forget to include a specific piece of information.
  C must try to get in touch with someone they know abroad.

3 **A** Jen's friends don't need to take anything to the party.
  B Jen's friends are having a party for her on Sunday.
  C Jen's friends are invited to Jen's for a special occasion.

4 **A** Meg wants Max to do something for her.
  B Max always fixes his sister's phone.
  C Max has not replied to Meg's texts.

5 **A** Pixie thinks sign language will be difficult to learn.
  B Pixie wants Charlotte to teach her sign language.
  C Pixie wants to use sign language with Charlotte.

✓ **EXAM TIPS**

- Understanding the purpose of the message will help you choose the correct answer.
- Make sure you know why the other options are incorrect.

3 **Match the highlighted words and phrases in the texts to the meanings.**

1 allowing people to compete
2 unable to hear
3 natural ability
4 a group of similar things

1 Write the words in the correct order to make reported questions.

0 whether / wondered / a text message / received / she / had
Jessica *wondered whether she had received a text message.*

1 what time / to / his mum / wanted / know / collecting / was / him
Billy _____ .

2 I / me / for breakfast / what / asked / wanted
Mum _____ .

3 to / the phone / we / had / know / wanted / if / finished chatting / on
Dad _____ .

4 cinema / the man / asked / which floor / the / on / was
The teenagers _____ .

5 if / I / picked up / wondered / the post office / had / her parcel / from
Ms March _____ .

2 Complete the reported questions. Make the necessary changes to pronouns, possessive adjectives and tenses.

1 'Are you ready to have dinner yet?'
Mum asked _____ ready to have dinner.

2 'Have you sent your aunt a text wishing her a happy birthday?'
Mum wanted to know _____ a text wishing her a happy birthday.

3 'Have you listened to me at all today?'
Mum asked _____ at all that day.

4 'Do you think you'll hand in your biology project on Wednesday?'
Mum wondered _____ my biology project on Wednesday.

5 'Will you watch a film on your computer later?'
Mum wanted to know _____ computer later.

6 'Would you like to go to the cinema instead?'
Mum wondered _____ the cinema instead.

7 'Do you want to go for a pizza after the film?'
Mum asked _____ for a pizza after the film.

3 Complete the conversation. Use the speech bubbles to help you.

> When did it happen?   How did it happen?
>
> Is he badly hurt?   Where is he now?

Julia: Dad, I told Michelle about Neil's accident. She asked [1] _____ .

Dad: I think it was the day before yesterday.

Julia: Oh, and also, she wanted to know [2] _____ .

Dad: Well, no one seems to know for sure.

Julia: She wondered [3] _____ .

Dad: Well, he broke his arm, but it wasn't a bad break.

Julia: Ah, so is he at home now? Michelle asked [4] _____ .

Dad: He's still in hospital, I think.

4 Correct the mistakes in these sentences or put a tick (✓) by any you think are correct.

1 They were new in our area and I want to know who they were.
_____

2 By chance, he was in the park and I said him if he would like to play.
_____

3 You wanted to know how was the new house.
_____

4 I asked her if I can take someone with me to the appointment.
_____

1 Choose the correct answer.

1 A: Did you see that programme about Facebook last night?
  B: No, I was *very / quite* busy – I had homework for three subjects to do for today.

2 A: How was the English test?
  B: It was *really / fairly* easy. I think I probably got about 60%.

3 A: What did you think of the restaurant?
  B: The meals were *reasonably / very* cheap, but not as cheap as I'd expected.

4 A: Did you like that book I lent you?
  B: It was *quite / very* good, but the ending was disappointing.

2 Put the adverb in brackets into the correct place in the sentence.

1 It was noisy in the restaurant, so I couldn't hear the musicians. (quite)

2 I didn't have any lunch, so I was feeling hungry by 3.00. (pretty)

3 On the whole, Dad kept calm when I told him the news. (reasonably)

4 Xanthe did well at school, but not as well as her brother. (quite)

WRITING   An article (2)

>> See *Prepare to write* box, Student's Book page 101.

1 Complete the phrases for saying what you think with the words in the box.

| may | opinion | say | think |

In my [1] _____
(Some/Many) people [2] _____ / think …
I don't [3] _____
Other people [4] _____ think …
but I think …

2 Write a sentence giving your opinion about the following.

1 Updating your social media status several times a day

2 Having thousands of friends on Facebook

3 Accepting friend requests from people you don't know

4 Looking at other people's web pages all the time

5 Being friends with your family online

PREPARE FOR THE EXAM

Writing Part 2 (An article)

3 Look at this exam task and make some notes to answer the questions below.

You see this notice on an English-language website.

Articles wanted!

Communication

What does it mean if someone is a good communicator?

How could you improve how you communicate?

How important is it to be able to communicate well with other people?

Write an interesting article answering these questions and we'll put it on our website soon!

4 Write your article.

- Use your notes from Exercise 3.
- Remember to check your spelling and grammar.
- Write about 100 words.

EXAM TIPS

- Make sure you do everything you are asked to do.
- Check your work carefully at the end.

VOCABULARY Personal feelings and qualities

1 Match the adjectives to their meanings.

1 annoyed	....	**a**	not expected
2 charming	....	**b**	making you feel worried and not able to relax
3 curious	....	**c**	quite angry
4 delighted	....	**d**	very pleased
5 lonely	....	**e**	wanting to know or learn about something
6 mad (about)	....	**f**	bad or unpleasant
7 nasty	....	**g**	unhappy because you aren't with other people
8 professional	....	**h**	showing skill and careful attention
9 rude	....	**i**	not confident, especially when meeting or talking to new people
10 shy	....	**j**	loving someone or something
11 stressful	....	**k**	pleasant and attractive
12 unexpected	....	**l**	not polite and upsetting other people

2 Read the situation and choose the two correct adjectives.

0 The singer got up, shouted at everyone and walked out. Everyone was shocked.
(rude)/ lonely /(unexpected)

1 That camerawoman is always on her own. She doesn't talk to anyone and she's very quiet.
lonely / charming / shy

2 The director we're working with is so nice. She's helpful and she's getting us to do some great work.
professional / annoyed / charming

3 I was the only person in our group, who did any work. It was hard and I'm not very happy about it.
annoyed / nasty / stressful

4 I just love sunglasses! Thank you so much for the present!
delighted / mad about / rude

5 I wanted to know what would happen in the end, so I read the last page and spoiled the story! I wish I hadn't!
annoyed / curious / shy

6 I can't believe the way that actor spoke to you.
nasty / rude / charming

3 Choose the correct answer.

1 Last week I had an *unexpected* / *annoyed* visit from my best friend, Billy. It was so nice.

2 The actress was *charming* / *shy*. She answered all the interview questions with a smile.

3 Martha is *nasty* / *mad* about that new boy band. She's always listening to their music.

4 The boy was *delighted* / *shy* with the new phone his parents gave him as a gift.

5 I was *rude* / *curious* to know what would happen next in the film.

6 The way that star spoke to the fan was just *stressful* / *rude*. She told him to go away.

4 Choose the correct adjectives from Exercise 1 to complete the article. More than one adjective may be possible.

Wanna be famous?

We asked three students this question. Here's what they said.

Emma, 15: 'I'd hate to be famous. I think I'd get really [1] _____ about being followed around everywhere by the paparazzi. I'm quite a [2] _____ person and don't like being the centre of attention, so not having a private life would be hard for me.'

Jan, 14: 'I'm not [3] _____ the idea of being famous and getting recognised everywhere you go – that would probably be fun for a while, but then you'd get sick of not being able to do anything without people wanting selfies with you. It would become [4] _____ I think, having to talk to everyone all the time, especially when you're tired or in a bad mood.'

Valentina, 13: 'Would I like to be famous? I don't think so. I actually think it would be quite a [5] _____ life because you'd have to hide away from journalists and fans all the time and you wouldn't be able to go out with your friends. And you'd have to cope with people writing [6] _____ comments about you on social media. No thanks!'

1 Read the article quickly. What does *siblings* mean?

1 famous people
2 people with famous brothers and sisters
3 brothers and sisters

CELEBRITY
SIBLINGS

Imagine how you'd feel if your brother's just brought home an Oscar and you've just got home from a shift in a fast food joint. Would you be annoyed by the difference in your lives? Delighted for his success? Perhaps a bit of both?

Having a world-famous brother or sister has its ups and downs. While your celebrity sister's having her nails done, being given a flash car, or walking round in free designer gear, you're doing your own make-up, riding around on an old bicycle and wondering whether you can afford a new pair of jeans!

This, according to psychologists, could cause what's known as 'sibling rivalry', or conflict between brothers and sisters. While this is normal in most families with siblings, and usually begins at a young age, it can be more of a problem in families where one sibling is a 'high achiever' and another is an 'underachiever'. This is a phenomenon which psychologists say is not uncommon.

Where there's a famous brother or sister in the mix, the 'ordinary' sibling may end up feeling lonely or upset about the attention their sibling receives, while they feel ignored. In the worst case, things can turn nasty, creating a stressful situation for the rest of the family. At this point, it's down to all the family members to show each other how much they value each sibling's achievements, no matter how 'big' or 'small'.

Rivalry, say psychologists, is really a waste of time. Everyone has their own unique set of qualities and weak points. OK, so your brother may be a 'household name', but that doesn't mean you've failed if you don't end up with a million followers on Twitter. The key is to work on achieving your own dreams, making the most of what *you* have to offer.

Of course, not everyone with a celebrity sibling feels bad about it. There can be moments where you feel incredibly proud of what your brother or sister has achieved. And there can be some unexpected benefits, too, such as being handed the designer gear that didn't fit or getting into gigs for free. You might even appear on the red carpet yourself in support of your sibling's new film or album, without the hassle of being asked for selfies and autographs. You can enjoy the good stuff without having to make any effort for it – perfect if you're naturally shy or just not mad about becoming famous yourself!

2 Read the article again and the questions below. Decide whether each statement is correct or incorrect. Write C for correct and I for incorrect.

The article says that
1 Brothers and sisters first become competitive when they are little. ....
2 Brothers and sisters from the same family are often as successful as each other. ....
3 Experts say that parents often create competition between siblings without realising. ....
4 Jealous feelings can sometimes actually be useful. ....
5 The best way to overcome feelings of jealousy is to think about your own skills. ....
6 The positives of having a celebrity brother or sister are greater than the negatives. ....

3 Match the highlighted words and phrases in the article to the meanings.

1 disagreement ....
2 something that exists or happens, often something unusual ....
3 someone or something that everyone knows ....
4 annoying because it is difficult or unpleasant to do ....
5 the mixture of good and bad things that happen

1 Complete the sentences, using the correct form of the words in brackets.

0 Maureen _____has her hair cut_____ by her friend. (hair / cut)

1 Mark _____ by the local bike shop. (bike / repair)

2 My mum _____ by the village baker last week. (my birthday cake / make)

3 Jeff _____ by a pavement artist every year. (picture / paint)

4 We _____ last year. (our house / paint)

5 Mum _____ by professional decorators. (her bedroom / decorate)

6 I _____ by the dentist. (a tooth / fill)

2 Rewrite the second sentence, using *have something done*.

0 This morning they parked my car outside the garage.
This morning I had my car parked outside the garage.

1 They took my picture yesterday.

2 They have cut and washed my hair.

3 They prepared the food for me.

4 They are going to make me a new jacket.

5 They have cleaned my shoes.

6 They are going to update our website.

3 Look at the pictures. What have the people had done? Use verbs from the box to write sentences.

~~cut~~	deliver	fix	repair	take

0 *He's had his hair cut very short.*

1 _____

2 _____

3 _____

4 _____

4 Choose the correct sentence in each pair.

1 a I was happy to see him there and I asked him to take a photo with me.
  b I was happy to see him there and I asked him to have his photo taken with me.

2 a What have you had done to your hair? It looks great!
  b What have you had made to your hair? It looks great!

3 a In Madame Tussauds, I had pictures with Tom Hardy and Meghan Markle!
  b In Madame Tussauds, I had pictures taken with Tom Hardy and Meghan Markle!

4 a I have to see the doctor and have my heart rate checked.
  b I have to see the doctor and have to check my heart rate.

1 Complete the sentences with *to*, *of* or *unless* if necessary. If no preposition is needed, write '–'.

1 According _____ Janet, it's going to rain tomorrow.
2 What do we need to take on the school trip besides _____ our lunch?
3 Despite _____ having two projects to do, I'm still going to watch the football!
4 My favourite singer is doing two concerts because _____ his huge number of fans.
5 I don't follow celebrity news _____ it's about my favourite footballer.
6 Let's study at your house tomorrow instead _____ mine.

PREPARE FOR THE EXAM

Reading Part 6

2 Read the article quickly. What kind of person is Hugh Jackman?

3 Read the article again and think of the word which best fits each gap. Use only one word in each gap. There is an example at the beginning.

HUGH JACKMAN

Hugh Jackman, star of *Wolverine* and *The Greatest Showman*, likes his fans. Instead ⁰ *of* ignoring them, he makes the effort to talk to them, and ¹ _____ of this, he's known as one of Hollywood's 'good guys'. It seems that ² _____ being world-famous, this Australian actor is still an ordinary person.

In 2016, a 9-year-old boy with a serious illness was on a radio show, sitting in the studio and asking Jackman questions in a phone interview. When he asked Jackman what his favourite line in *Wolverine* was, ³ _____ of answering him, Jackman came into the room himself and gave the boy the answer! They said a few lines from the film together and ⁴ _____ to the actor, the boy became one of his favourite fans.

⁵ _____ this, Jackman helped a singer in *The Greatest Showman* feel less nervous by holding her hand. ⁶ _____ he's using his acting skills to pretend to be nice (we're sure he isn't!), Hugh Jackman's a really good guy!

EXAM TIPS

- Read the words before and after each gap before you decide which word to write.
- Often the first word you think of is the correct one. Complete the text, then check your answers to make sure the text makes sense.

1 Read the questions in Exercise 2. What is the topic of the interview?

PREPARE FOR THE EXAM

Listening Part 4

2 You will hear an interview with a reporter called Ignacio Mendes. For each question, choose the correct answer. Then listen again and check your answers.

09

1 Ignacio says that many people think celebrities
  A do nothing useful for society.
  B are paid too much for what they do.
  C are too confident about their abilities.
2 Ignacio says that the celebrities he has met
  A do not particularly enjoy being famous.
  B are often very ordinary people.
  C have a lot of ambitions.
3 When asked about the difference between celebrities and being famous, Ignacio says
  A he disagrees with how the word celebrity is defined.
  B he thinks that people of any profession can be famous.
  C he believes journalists have the power to make people famous.
4 Ignacio thinks the most important thing celebrities do is
  A provide people with entertainment.
  B encourage people to develop their talents.
  C help people find out about world issues.
5 Ignacio says he particularly respects celebrities who
  A make time to meet their fans.
  B give a lot of money to charity.
  C prefer to stay out of public view.
6 Ignacio says that becoming a celebrity himself would make him feel
  A excited about how he could help other people.
  B stressed about being watched all the time.
  C nervous about whether he was good at his job.

EXAM TIPS

- Read the questions and options and think carefully about what they mean.
- You may hear words in the recording which you see in the questions. Be careful! The option which contains the word you hear may not be the right answer.

19 THE WORLD OF WORK

VOCABULARY | Work tasks

1 Match the words in the box to their meanings.

arrange	calculate	deal with	deliver	develop	handle
install	manage	organise	produce	run	update

1 add new information
2 take things such as goods, letters and parcels to people's homes or places of work
3 control something, e.g. an event
4 discover an amount or number using maths
5 plan or prepare for something
6 make the necessary plans for something to happen
7 be in control of an office, shop or team
8 make something new over time
9 make or grow something
10 put a piece of equipment somewhere and make it ready for use
11 take action in order to achieve something or in order to solve a problem
12 understand and take action in a difficult situation

2 Read the sentences and choose the two correct answers.

1 Jason's dad *runs / manages / produces* a small Thai restaurant in our town.
2 Mr McKenzie had to *calculate / deal with / manage* a large number of complaints about the new school café.
3 I thought Mr McKenzie *handled / dealt with / organised* the problems with the homework really well.
4 The IT people are coming next week to *update / install / arrange* the school computer system.
5 Who is going to *calculate / produce / update* our class blog this week?

3 Complete the blog post with these verbs from Exercise 1.

calculate	deal	deliver	develop	install	manage	organise

Guys, guess what!! I got the holiday job. I'm so excited! The woman who runs the shop – Mrs Ford – asked me when I could start work! It's going to be great – I have to ¹ .... with people, ² .... newspapers to a few homes and ³ .... some orders – you know, work out how many things we need and how much they cost.

Mrs Ford asked me if I could ⁴ .... some upgrades to her computer (easy!) and then she wants me to help ⁵ .... a new website.

Also, we're going to ⁶ .... a healthy milkshake afternoon (so, no sugar!) for the primary school kids, when they get off the school bus. I'm excited! I'll have to ⁷ .... my time really well.

Posted by Marina on Monday at 2.02pm

READING

 PREPARE FOR THE EXAM

Reading Part 2

1 The people below all want to find a job for the summer holidays. Read the texts and decide what kind of job you think would suit each person.

1 Jennie loves maths and reading and would love to work somewhere where she can spend time doing both things. She would like a quiet kind of job, where she can work on her own.

2 Mason enjoys being active and spends lots of time in the gym. He'd like to work in a different kind of environment to this and enjoys meeting interesting people.

3 Bianca likes organising projects and is happy to be in an office, working as part of a team. She also enjoys good food and social occasions.

4 Connor enjoys helping other people learn to do things and he is very patient. He has great IT skills and would like the chance to try to improve them.

5 Hannah is a very lively person who likes everything about history. She feels very confident talking to groups of people and enjoys learning.

2 Here are eight advertisements for holiday jobs. Decide which job would be most suitable for the people in Exercise 1.

HOLIDAY JOBS

A CLIFTON LIBRARY
We need a support assistant to work in our computer room. Members of the public can use the computers for free and often have questions about how to do things. We need someone who's calm and enjoys showing people how to solve problems. You will attend relevant computer training courses and also have access to our specialist reference library for staff.

B MARCO'S HAIR
Join us in our busy salon as a receptionist and help keep our appointment system up-to-date. Your tasks will involve answering the phone, managing the diary and greeting customers when they arrive, as well as ordering products. You'll receive great pay and get free haircuts!

C THE STUDIO
We're looking for an events officer who will help make sure all our events go smoothly. We need someone who's good at managing lots of tasks at the same time, and who doesn't mind being at a desk with other people on the same project. We run a wide variety of events at The Studio, from concerts to dining experiences, which you will have the chance to attend!

D JONES PUBLISHING
Jones Publishing needs an assistant to help in the accounts department. The right person should be happy working alone on tasks and must be good with numbers. For those with good English skills, there's also the chance to review new books and post opinions of them on our website.

 EXAM TIPS

- You may find similar information in different options. Make sure you understand what each person is looking for.
- There is only one option, which fits each person correctly.

3 Match the **highlighted** words in the advertisements to the meanings.

1 eating ....
2 happen without problems or difficulties ....
3 the quality of being strong ....
4 a shop where you can have your hair cut ....
5 at the moment ....

E FACTORY FOODS
Factory foods make prepared meals for sale in supermarkets. We currently have positions available for people to work in our factory, packing goods ready for transport. Jobs may involve working on your own in one area of the store and doing some heavy lifting.

F GECKO TOURS
Are you fun and friendly? Would you be happy holding meetings with our tour guides telling them about places you've spent time researching and which we'd like to include in our historical tours? We'd love to hear from anyone who loves finding out about new things and informing other people about what they've discovered.

G THE BOLD HOTEL
The Bold Hotel needs porters to help greet guests as they arrive and take care of their luggage. We're looking for someone fit enough to be able to lift heavy items, as well as someone who's friendly and confident. We receive guests from all over the world, who have great stories to tell. No experience necessary.

H CITY MUSEUM
We have lots of exhibitions on this summer and require help setting up the displays. This will give you the chance to find out about our interesting collections. Some strength is required for moving larger items. You'll work in a large team and will not be required to talk to the visitors.

1 Choose the two correct linking words or phrases.

1 I have to go to bed earlier *as / because / while* I have to catch an early bus tomorrow.
2 Matthew never took notes in class, *although / in order to / whereas* his brother took lots.
3 I need to put on my glasses *so that I can / because / in order to* read this form.
4 She seems really easygoing, *while / whereas / because* she's actually pretty difficult.
5 I can pick up some milk *although / as / because* I'm going past the shops on my way home.
6 Last year I went to the USA *in order to / so that I could / because* go to my cousin's wedding.

2 Complete the sentences with the beginnings or endings below. Use *although*, *as* or *so that* to join the two parts.

> your work will be mainly in the shop
> I enjoyed the party
> I'm not going to have a starter
> the teacher can explain the rules to you
> I have football practice
> ~~she can improve her grades~~

0 She's going to study harder
   so that she can improve her grades .
1 _____ I didn't know anyone.
2 You should arrive earlier on the first day _____ .
3 _____ we might need you in the café too.
4 _____ I want to have a dessert!
5 I'll be home late tonight _____ .

3 Complete the blog post with the correct linking word(s) from the box. More than one may be possible.

> as   because   in order to   so that   whereas (x2)

I have the best job in the world! But I'm not going to say what it is
¹ _____ this is a game and you have to guess.
I'll give you a few clues ² _____ you can work
it out. It wouldn't be a fun job for someone who didn't like dealing
with customers, especially little kids. I usually work at the beach and
³ _____ have something to eat and get cool, you'll
probably come and visit me. Some people know what they want and
they choose from 100 flavours quickly, ⁴ _____
others can take forever to decide! You're on holiday and have all the
time in the world, ⁵ _____ I'm working and time
is money!

What's my job? Post your answers!

4 Correct the mistakes in these sentences or put a tick (✓) by any you think are correct.

1 They gave me a gift while I left my job.
2 We hope you can send us the figures that we can complete the project.
3 You have to prepare for your exams so to get the qualifications you need.
4 I enjoyed the job because I met some really interesting people.
5 I like Stefanie while she is a very kind, friendly and confident person.

1 Read about these jobs and complete the text with *as* or *like*.

1 There are lots of young people who are working _____ bloggers. They write about things that interest them _____ fashion or food. The experience of writing online, having followers and reading other people's posts can be excellent experience for many jobs _____ writing for a newspaper.
2 I work in a high street shop on Saturday mornings. It's OK, but I'd like to do something more interesting _____ my friend Luis, who works at the library. He says it's boring, but I think it would be wonderful to work _____ a junior librarian because I love books! I'm known in my school _____ *Bookie* because I read so many books!

>> See *Prepare to write* box, Student's Book page 111.

1 Below is a list of tasks that you might have to do in a part-time job. Write a job from the box or add your own idea next to each task.

| hairdresser's assistant | newspaper boy/girl |
| shop assistant | working in a café/restaurant |

1 organising the shelves
2 making an appointment
3 calculating the change to give a customer
4 dealing with enquiries
5 delivering goods
6 making a reservation
7 developing social media
8 handling difficult customers
9 cleaning the floor
10 serving customers
11 organising an event
12 updating an advertisement

2 Read Elise's email and Ethan's reply. Were all of her questions answered?

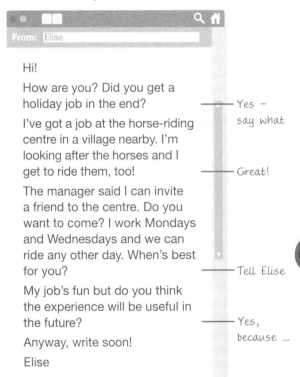

From: Elise

Hi!

How are you? Did you get a holiday job in the end? —— Yes – say what

I've got a job at the horse-riding centre in a village nearby. I'm looking after the horses and I get to ride them, too! —— Great!

The manager said I can invite a friend to the centre. Do you want to come? I work Mondays and Wednesdays and we can ride any other day. When's best for you? —— Tell Elise

My job's fun but do you think the experience will be useful in the future? —— Yes, because ...

Anyway, write soon!

Elise

Hi Elise,

Thanks for your email! Yes, I got a holiday job as a waiter at the café in town. The people are friendly and I enjoy working there.

Your job sounds great! I know how much you love horses and riding.

I'd love to come riding at the centre with you. I work on Tuesdays, Thursdays and Saturdays, so why don't we go riding one Friday?

I think your job will be useful in future because it shows that you can be responsible.

See you soon!

Ethan

3 Read this email you have received from your friend Kyle. Look at the notes and plan what you will say. Make brief notes. Think about:

what you will say about Kyle's job
why you can't go to the cinema next week
what you will say about your job at the theatre
what you could write in a CV about both your jobs.

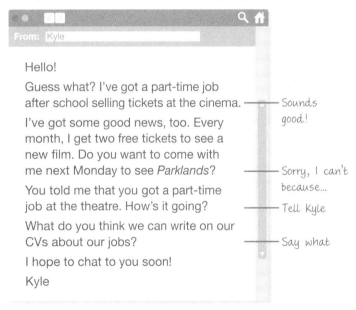

From: Kyle

Hello!

Guess what? I've got a part-time job after school selling tickets at the cinema. —— Sounds good!

I've got some good news, too. Every month, I get two free tickets to see a new film. Do you want to come with me next Monday to see *Parklands*? —— Sorry, I can't because...

You told me that you got a part-time job at the theatre. How's it going? —— Tell Kyle

What do you think we can write on our CVs about our jobs? —— Say what

I hope to chat to you soon!

Kyle

 PREPARE FOR THE EXAM

Writing Part 1

5 Write your email to Kyle, using all the notes.

- Write in an informal style.
- Write about 100 words.
- Remember to check your spelling and grammar.

EXAM TIPS

- Make sure you have used ALL the notes.
- When you have finished writing, check your answer carefully for correct spelling and grammar.

20 MAKING PLANS

VOCABULARY · Hopes and dreams

1 Find the words in the word square (→↓↗) to match the meanings.

1 succeed in something good, usually by working hard

2 find someone or something attractive or impressive

3 intend to do something

4 decide to do something

5 think of something that you would like to happen

6 make someone more likely to do something or make them more confident

7 have an idea of something in your mind

8 make the greatest effort possible

d	h	y	r	l	p	q	f	e	b	s	z
o	y	h	k	m	f	a	v	g	d	w	t
i	m	a	g	i	n	e	j	x	r	s	c
k	p	h	o	y	i	l	w	r	e	n	b
k	e	t	s	h	c	v	y	b	a	s	g
e	d	b	c	g	h	w	r	a	m	m	i
e	z	a	i	m	o	u	u	l	p	h	f
p	m	d	j	l	o	f	a	b	t	r	d
o	o	m	i	y	s	s	o	x	p	h	f
n	l	i	y	e	e	n	l	r	k	s	g
z	c	r	b	o	k	l	t	e	v	m	q
f	t	e	n	c	o	u	r	a	g	e	i

2 Choose the correct answer.

1 My grandfather *dreamt* / *chose* of being an airline pilot.

2 I *encourage* / *aim* to go to university and study history.

3 Who do you think has *achieved* / *admired* more – the inventors of Google or Facebook?

4 Michelle *admired* / *imagined* Steve for his amazing guitar-playing skills.

5 This boy at school has *achieved* / *encouraged* me to join the basketball team practice on Fridays.

6 We told our teacher that we had *kept on* / *tried our best* at the athletics competition.

7 Next year we have to *choose* / *aim* which subjects to do for the exams.

8 Older people can't *aim* / *imagine* how hard we have to study these days.

3 Read this talk that a teacher is giving his class just before the end-of-year exams. Complete it with the correct form of the verbs from Exercise 1.

OK, class. Listen, everybody! Before the exams start on Monday I just want to say a few things. I guess that you are all [1] _____ of getting good marks? Well, you may be, but it's just as important to [2] _____ in everything you do. Here are some ideas to help you revise. First, I would [3] _____ you to write out a plan for the subject you're studying and then find a quiet place to work. If I were you, I'd [4] _____ to study for about three hours at a time, but have a break every 20 minutes or so. Not many of us can keep studying for longer. I [5] _____ people who can concentrate for long periods, but most of us need a rest from time to time! If you find that you are unable to [6] _____ much, then try not to worry. Have a break and come back to it feeling fresh. Then you'll be able to carry on. Try to [7] _____ yourself holding that piece of paper with your exam result on – it reads 'excellent', right? It's up to you – you just have to [8] _____ to succeed.

1 Read the title of the article quickly. What do Adam and Ellie do?

2 Look at the sentences below. Read the article and decide if each sentence is correct or incorrect. Write C for correct and I for incorrect.

1 Adam was not keen on doing jobs on the farm. ....
2 Adam's best friend had a dog that Adam used to take for walks. ....
3 Adam thought of the idea for his business when he helped someone who lived nearby. ....
4 Adam was unable to start his business while he lived on the farm. ....
5 Adam found it easy to run his business at first. ....
6 Ellie was not able to follow one of her dreams. ....
7 Ellie and Adam run similar kinds of business. ....
8 Both Adam and Ellie were helped by their families. ....
9 Ellie felt excited about teaching young children at first. ....
10 Both Adam's and Ellie's businesses are now going well. ....

SUCCESS STORIES

Want to be inspired to set up your own business? We spoke to two teenagers who already have.

Adam had always dreamt of working with animals. 'I grew up on a farm, where I was involved with feeding the cows and cleaning the shed where they lived in winter. I didn't mind helping out,' he says. 'We also had a pet dog called Zen, who was a great friend. He would wait for me to come home from school every day, and then I'd take him for a long walk in the woods.'

There were a few older people in the village who had dogs that needed walks, but who couldn't take them very far. One of them asked Adam if he would walk her dog, and once he'd agreed, other people started asking, too. 'I didn't ask for any money, but it gave me an idea for a business – dog-walking!' says Adam. But since he couldn't do any more in the place where he lived, he forgot about it for a few years.

When Adam was thirteen, his family sold the farm and moved to a town where his parents set up their own business. That encouraged Adam to do the same, and he remembered his dog-walking idea. 'My parents helped me print leaflets advertising my services, and suggested a price I could ask. On the first day I received so many calls that I didn't know how to deal with them all!' Adam says. Adam's mother set up a diary for him on her computer and the business quickly became successful. 'Now I aim to employ someone to help me walk the dogs after school!' says Adam.

Another young person who set up their own business is Ellie, aged fifteen. 'I've loved athletics since I was a kid,' she says. 'I hoped to get to the Olympics but I'm not good enough. I thought about giving up.' But Ellie's grandmother believed in her ability to be successful in athletics, even if she couldn't compete at a high level. She encouraged Ellie to keep on training, and when a local sports club was looking for volunteers to help train children, she suggested that Ellie offered to help.

Ellie considered the idea and decided to give it a try. 'I never imagined I'd be a good teacher, but the minute I got on the field and realised how excited the kids were, I knew it was the right thing for me.' Since then, Ellie has set up her own one-to-one athletics training programme and has ten young people who she trains after school. 'I love it!' she says.

Good luck, Adam and Ellie!

3 Match the **highlighted** words in the article to the meanings.

1 a plan of activities with a purpose ....
2 a folded piece of paper which contains information ....
3 pay someone to work for a business ....
4 do things and be part of an activity or event ....
5 think carefully about a decision ....

Verbs with two objects

1 Add *to* or *for* in the correct place in these sentences.

0 I sent the text *to* the wrong person.

1 Stephanie wrote a letter the newspaper.

2 Mum bought a book of poetry me.

3 The boys gave a big box of chocolates their father.

4 Alina and Margie showed their holiday photos their friends.

5 The grandparents told a story their grandchildren every night.

2 Write the words in the correct order to make sentences.

1 secret / best / me / My / told / a / friend

2 surprise / present / gave / My / me / a / parents

3 showed / new / us / Mum / dress / her / to

4 shoes / bought / I / myself / a pair / of / expensive

5 sent / a book / to / Mark / his / parents

6 The / wrote / parents / a letter / teacher / to / the

3 Read the text and answer the questions in full.

1 What had Sara's friends sent her?

2 What did Sara's parents give her?

3 Who had sent Sara the envelope?

4 Who told Sara a story?

5 What did they do in the end?

4 Complete the second sentence in each pair, so that it means the same as the first.

1 They brought a small present for me.
They brought me _____

2 Josh gave a party invitation to Lucy.
Josh _____

3 Mr Digby sent his students an email.
Mr Digby _____

4 Jason took the girl some flowers.
Jason _____

5 Millie showed the picture to her friends.
Millie _____

6 The class gave the boy a prize.
The class _____

5 Correct the mistakes in these sentences or put a tick (✓) by any you think are correct.

1 I want to introduce you all my friends.

2 I tell to her all my secrets.

3 She lent him the money because he promised to give it back to her soon.

4 When she arrived at school, all her classmates sang 'Happy birthday to you!' and gave to her a lot of presents.

5 Together, we baked some cakes to our friends.

It was Sara's birthday and she woke up early to see that her phone had been busy through the night! Lots of friends had sent her birthday wishes. As she went downstairs, she heard Mum and Dad talking softly to each other and then she saw a huge box in front of them. Dad looked at her and said 'Happy Birthday Sara. Here's your present.' She had no idea what it was. 'It must be something big,' she thought! She opened each layer of paper and there was another box, and then another and another. Finally, she reached the bottom – and there was an envelope with a stamp on it. It was from her grandmother in Australia. As she opened it she saw the words 'London–Sydney' – it was a plane ticket! She couldn't believe it! She was going to visit her grandmother in Sydney! Mum told her the story of how they had planned the surprise in secret. It was the best present ever. They took a photo of Sara smiling with her ticket and sent it to Grandma immediately.

VOCABULARY Phrasal verbs

1 Choose the correct prepositions.

1 Do you believe *in / for* luck?
2 I don't know if I can go to the party – it depends *with / on* what my parents say.
3 I need to work *out / for* what I want to do after I leave school. I've got no idea!
4 I'm going to go *in / for* that babysitting job.
5 Harry never joins *into / in* sports games.
6 Maggie got *for / into* college. She's excited about starting her new course.
7 I'm going to keep *to / on* going to drama club. I might be a famous actor one day!
8 I missed *in / out* on getting a free gift at the exhibition because I arrived too late.

2 Complete the notice with the correct form of the verbs from the box.

believe	get	go	join	keep

NATIONAL TEAM SELECTION!

Congratulations to Harry Rowe and Jessica Ambleside! We always ¹ _____ in you and now you have both ² _____ into the national basketball teams. We are very proud of you. We know that you will have to practise a lot and ³ _____ on working really hard, but we hope that you will still be able to ⁴ _____ in regular school activities. Just ⁵ _____ for it and have fun!

LISTENING

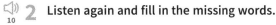

1 You will hear the first part of a conversation between two teenagers talking about an idea for a business. Tick (✓) the topics they mention.

what the business is ☐
managing the product ☐
how they had the idea for the product ☐
what the product is ☐
similar products available ☐
their friends' opinions ☐

2 Listen again and fill in the missing words.

Craig: So, Kathy, what do you think about ¹ _____ up our own business?

Kathy: I'm not sure. Do you think that our homemade fruit juices are *that* good?

Craig: Everyone at school ² _____ them and you said that your parents loved them. I think we have a great idea, and ³ _____ else has done it. A fruit juice in a bag!

Kathy: I know, Craig, but that was only because we didn't have any paper cups ⁴ _____ ! But that's how all the great ideas start, isn't it? People make a ⁵ _____ for themselves with crazy ideas or have ideas just because something strange happened. That could be us! So, what should we call them? Bag of fruit? Fruit in a bag?

3 Answer the questions.

1 What is the product?

2 Who likes it?

3 How did they get the idea?

4 What are they going to call it?

4 Look at the six sentences. Listen to the whole conversation and decide if each sentence is correct or incorrect. If it is correct, choose the letter A. If it is not correct, choose the letter B.

1 Craig believes that they have an unusual idea. **A B**
2 Kathy thinks they may become famous. **A B**
3 Craig and Kathy agree to put their idea online. **A B**
4 Craig suggests all the photos should be taken indoors. **A B**
5 Kathy thinks people will enjoy the product in many places. **A B**
6 Craig thinks that they should show good-looking people in their advertising. **A B**

Acknowledgements

The authors and publishers acknowledge the following sources of copyright material and are grateful for the permissions granted. While every effort has been made, it has not always been possible to identify the sources of all the material used, or to trace all copyright holders. If any omissions are brought to our notice, we will be happy to include the appropriate acknowledgements on reprinting and in the next update to the digital edition, as applicable.

Key: U = Unit.

Text
U11: Mail Online for the adapted text from 'The World's Biggest School' by Daily Mail Reporter, *Mail Online*, 23.08.2013. Copyright © 2013 Mail Online. All rights reserved. Distributed by Solo Syndication; **U15**: First News for the adapted text from 'How much time do you spend outside?' by First News Reporter, *First News*, 11.04.2014. Copyright © 2014 First Group Enterprises Ltd. Reproduced with kind permission; **U20**: United Church of God for the adapted text from 'Teenage stories: yours could start today' by Kae Tattersall, *The Good News*. Copyright © United Church of God. Reproduced with kind permission.

Photography
The following images are sourced from Getty Images.

U1: kali9/E+; aiqingwang/iStock Unreleased; pixelfit/iStock/ Getty Images Plus; **U2**: Hero Images; pixelfit/E+; kali9/iStock/ Getty Images Plus; Johner Images; Britt Erlanson/Cultura/ Getty Images Plus; fstop123/E+; Erik Isakson/Blend Images; fstop123/E+; **U3**: moodboard/Cultura; Steve Debenport/ iStock/Getty Images Plus; Rayman/Photodisc; wihteorchid/ E+; garymilner/E+; Chuck Eckert/Photographer's Choice RF; David Madison/Photographer's Choice RF; Westend61; Luc Beziat/Photographer's Choice; **U4**: Gene Rhoden/Weatherpix/ Photolibrary; PickStock/E+; Harald Sund/Photographer's Choice; ArtwayPics/iStock Editorial/Getty Images Plus; oversnap/ iStock Unreleased; CHRISsadowski/iStock/Getty Images Plus; mokee81/iStock/Getty Images Plus; **U5**: Kittipong Ruangroj/ EyeEm; SebastianGauert/iStock/Getty Images Plus; **U6**: Poike/ iStock/Getty Images Plus; ValentynVolkov/iStock/Getty Images Plus; Elenathewise/iStock/Getty Images Plus; **U7**: lisegagne/E+; xijian/E+; **U8**: Franck-Boston/iStock/Getty Images Plus; Veronica Garbutt/Lonely Planet Images; Morsa Images/DigitalVision; Tim Robberts/DigitalVision; Plume Creative/DigitalVision; Dear Blue/ Moment; Hero Images; **U9**: Hero Images; Ulzanna/iStock/Getty Images Plus; alexsl/iStock/Getty Images Plus; BallBall14/iStock/ Getty Images Plus; skegbydave/E+; privilege84/iStock/Getty Images Plus; **U10**: Volker Schlichting/EyeEm; **U11:** Hero Images; STRDEL/Stringer/AFP; Gideon Mendel/Corbis; **U12:** gk-6mt/ iStock/Getty Images Plus; Dennis K. Johnson/Lonely Planet Images; Jon Feingersh/Blend Images; Holger Leue/Lonely Planet Images; Tetra Images; Compassionate Eye Foundation/ Robert Kent/DigitalVision; Stígur Már Karlsson/Heimsmyndir/ E+; Perboge; **U13:** luanateutzi/iStock/Getty Images Plus; Cultura RM Exclusive/Matelly/Cultura Exclusive; Kalulu/iStock/Getty Images Plus; golero/E+; **U14:** PhotoAlto/Eric Audras/PhotoAlto Agency RF Collections; **U15:** Jesse Kraft/EyeEm; Grant Faint/ Photolibrary; Tony Hopewell/DigitalVision; Harvepino/iStock/ Getty Images Plus; **U16:** Marc Romanelli/Blend Images; ollo/ iStock Unreleased; izusek/E+; **U17:** Jupiterimages/Photolibrary; **U18**: Tim Robberts/The Image Bank; Eri Morita/The Image Bank; Oliver Rossi/Corbis; Compassionate Eye Foundation/ Martin Barraud/Tax; Christopher Polk/ACMA2014/Getty Images Entertainment; CommerceandCultureAgency/Taxi; Dave J Hogan/Getty Images Entertainment; **U19**: True Art/EyeEm; Bloom Productions/Taxi; Alberto Guglielmi; Eri Morita/Photodisc; Ian Taylor/Design Pics/First Light; Rob Lewine; Alex Potemkin/E+; DragonImages/iStock/Getty Images Plus; **U20**: Cavan Images; FS-Stock/iStock/Getty Images Plus; David Oliver/Taxi; Brad Wilson/Stockbyte; Andy Crawford/Dorling Kindersley.

The following photographs have been sourced from other library/sources.

U7: Photopat vintage/Alamy Stock Photo; **U10**: Gillmar/ Shutterstock; Henrik Winther Andersen/Alamy Stock Photo; EMprize/Shutterstock; Suzanne Long/Alamy Stock Photo; Momanuma/Shutterstock; Gallo Images/Alamy Stock Photo; JLImages/Alamy Stock Photo; FloridaStock/Shutterstock.

Front cover photography by fanjianhua/Moment/Getty Images.

Illustration
Ludovic Salle (Advocate Art); Alex Sotirovski (Beehive Illustration); Mark Duffin.

The publishers are grateful to the following contributors: author of *Cambridge English Prepare! First Edition* Level 5 Workbook: Niki Joseph; cover design and design concept: restless; typesetting: emc design Ltd; audio recordings: produced by Leon Chambers and recorded at The SoundHouse Studios, London